M000158739

The

CONSCIENCE
MAN

The CONSCIENCE of MAN

DR. BILL SMITH

CREATION
HOUSE
A STRANG COMPANY

THE CONSCIENCE OF MAN by Dr. Bill Smith
Published by Creation House
A Strang Company
600 Rinehart Road
Lake Mary, Florida 32746
www.strangbookgroup.com

Unless otherwise noted, all Scripture quotations are from the King James Version of the Bible.

Bible verses marked GENEVA are from the Geneva Bible, 1599 edition.

Greek definitions are derived from *Strong's Exhaustive Concordance of the Bible*, ed. James Strong, Nashville, TN: Thomas Nelson Publishers, 1997.

Design Director: Bill Johnson
Cover Designer: Amanda Potter
Interior Designer: Annette Simpson

Library of Congress Control Number: 2009922338
International Standard Book Number: 978-1-59979-725-0

09 10 11 12 13 — 9 8 7 6 5 4 3 2
Printed in the United States of America

ACKNOWLEDGMENTS

I WOULD LIKE TO thank Pearl Cook, Peggy Teague, and Donna Russell for their help in proofreading, typing, editing, re-editing, and with the layout of this manuscript. Because of their talents and abilities, this book will be a blessing to thousands throughout the world.

CONTENTS

vii

PREFACE

WE ALL LIVE with our conscience, but few people understand its power of guidance and its ability to bring us into fellowship with God. The reason for this may be that the church has had little teaching on the conscience. When I began to understand what the Lord revealed on this subject, I realized that following our conscience always brings us to being led by the Spirit of God.

As a student of the apostle Paul, I found that Paul checked his conscience daily throughout his life. The Bible tells us in Acts 23:1, "And Paul, earnestly beholding the council, said, Men and brethren, I have lived in all good conscience before God until this day." Few people are able to say what Paul said in that verse. We can now understand why Paul was given so much revelation.

Maybe you are wondering where Paul's conscience was when he was killing Christians. We find the answer in the Bible. We are told his conscience was seared. Many Christians today find themselves with a seared conscience. They have become hardened and insensitive to the truth. If you are stuck spiritually and cannot find out why, this book will be a great help to you. I thank God for my conscience.

—DR. BILL SMITH

1

YOUR GOD-GIVEN CONSCIENCE

OST PEOPLE HAVE never heard or read a teaching about man's conscience. In fact, some people are what we call "free thinkers." This type of people tries to do away with their consciences altogether. We presently live in a time when humanism seems to be a way of life for some people. Humanists are those who believe, "If it feels good, do it. If you like it, do it." But these types of thoughts and beliefs are not what God has in mind for man.

When God created man, He created him with a conscience. From the most primitive tribes to the most sophisticated people, all that are born of Adam have a conscience. So that man's conscience might be renewed and purged of dead works, God gave us His Son (Jesus) as Lord and Savior and His indwelling Holy Spirit. We find this blessing of a renewed conscience in the book of Hebrews:

But Christ being come an high priest of good things to come, by a greater and more perfect tabernacle, not made with hands, that is to say, not of this building; Neither by the blood of goats and calves, but by his own blood he entered in once into the holy place, having obtained eternal redemption for us. For if the blood of bulls and of goats, and the ashes of an heifer sprinkling the unclean, sanctifieth to the purifying of

3

the flesh: How much more shall the blood of Christ, who through the eternal Spirit offered himself without spot to God, purge your conscience from dead works to serve the living God?

—HEBREWS 9:11–14

When you receive Christ as your Savior, God begins a work in you through His Son Jesus and His Holy Spirit. God renews your conscience, causing it to become alive. He removes that old, stony heart and replaces it with a new heart. He then establishes His salvation in your new heart. He places His Spirit and His Word within you, causing you to become changed into His image from glory to glory ever changing. It's a wondrous and blessed process by the hand of God.

IGNORANCE OF THE CONSCIENCE

For centuries people have tried to get away from the conscience by trying to ignore it. Today there are people who teach that your conscience means nothing. However, God does not say this at all. Our conscience is tied to the written Word of God. It will speak from the Word and the Holy Spirit every time. Without the conscience we have no anchor—no anchor at all. Because our conscience is from God, it will never be in conflict with His Word.

Through creation you and I bear the image of God. Although we lost much in the fall of man, the Bible maintains that all unregenerate people—(men and women)—are in revolt against the light of their conscience and nature. Whether a person is saved or lost, his conscience will bear witness to every sin, "For all have sinned and come short of the glory of God" (Rom. 3:23).

4

The first chapter of the Book of Romans is written about lost people. Beginning at verse 17, we see that nature and man's conscience are both aware of the holy God and His expectations of man.

For therein is the righteousness of God revealed from faith to faith: as it is written, The just shall live by faith. For the wrath of God is revealed from heaven against all ungodliness and unrighteousness of men, who hold the truth in unrighteousness; Because that which may be known of God is manifest in them; for God hath shewed it unto them. For the invisible things of him from the creation of the world are clearly seen, being understood by the things that are made, even his eternal power and Godhead; so that they are without excuse: Because that, when they knew God, they glorified him not as God, neither were thankful; but became vain in their imaginations, and their foolish heart was darkened. Professing themselves to be wise, they became fools, And changed the glory of the uncorruptible God into an image made like to corruptible man, and to birds, and fourfooted beasts, and creeping things. Wherefore God also gave them up to uncleanness through the lusts of their own hearts, to dishonour their own bodies between themselves: Who changed the truth of God into a lie, and worshipped and served the creature more than the Creator, who is blessed for ever. Amen. For this cause God gave them up unto vile affections: for even their women did change the natural use into that which is against nature.

—ROMANS 1:17–26

The first chapter of Romans continues to say the people had knowledge that their sinful ways were against God. They

5

knew better. They were aware of the judgment of God for the sins they had committed. (See Romans 1:32.) How were they made aware of their sins against God? Their conscience, which is God-created, told them what was wrong and what was right. Ignorance cannot be used as an excuse because we all have a conscience. Your conscience will always guide you through. God has said in His Word that all lost people know right from wrong and good from evil. (See Genesis 3:2 and Romans 2:14–16.)

Martin Luther wrote, "It is neither safe nor honest to do anything against the conscience. Here I stand, I can do no more."[1] Martin Luther stresses something very important in the words *here I stand, I can do no more.* Each of us is responsible for our own actions. Others cannot be held responsible for what we do, say, or think. A pastor can lead us or an elder can guide us, but they are not responsible for what we ultimately may or may not do. We are free moral agents for the Lord and are held accountable accordingly. The Bible says we all shall be judged for the deeds done in the body. We shall stand before the judgment seat of Christ.

TRUST YOUR CONSCIENCE

With God's law of sowing and reaping, Jesus taught man how to trust his conscience. The conscience always speaks to us when we sow that which is wrong. Even with the most primitive people, their consciences show them right from wrong. However, many primitive people fight their conscience because they view it as something negative rather than something positive. It is important for us to understand that our conscience shows us right from wrong and good from evil. Never expect God to give you the next step until you have obeyed your conscience. The reason is that if

6

you refuse to obey your conscience, you will also refuse to obey the Holy Spirit. Your conscience and the Holy Spirit are linked together very closely. God created us all in this way.

By now you may be asking, What is the conscience? Your conscience is similar to having another eye, another entity within you, or a second personality, if you prefer to describe it that way. Your conscience passes objective judgment upon your subjective life. The conscience is the part of you that makes it seem you are standing on the outside of your physical body watching yourself and knowing what you are saying, doing, and thinking. Your conscience passes judgment on you during and after whatever you say, think, or do. Yet, it is all subjective because your conscience is within you.

History tells us that men such as Socrates and Aristotle knew about man's conscience and its function. Socrates, (the Greek philosopher and teacher) called his conscience a "divine voice" that he had heard since his infancy.[1] Maybe he needed it. Maybe his life was one that he could not escape. Aristotle believed that inside man was a ruling faculty that distinguished him from beasts; it made him different from animals.

In the Old Testament we see the conscience at work. When Adam and Eve sinned they hid from God. The King James Version of the Bible says they were afraid and hid themselves. The literal Hebrew translation says, "Their heart smote them and they hid themselves" (Gen. 3:10). Have you ever had your heart smite you? As soon as we enter into sin, our heart smites us and we recognize we are wrong.

OLD TESTAMENT TEACHING

The Old Testament is a wonderful teacher about the conscience of man. We find many who were smitten by the problems in their hearts. A good example is in 1 Samuel 24:5. We find King Saul chasing David throughout the countryside trying to kill him. Because a messenger tells David where King Saul is camping, David decides to take some men with him and enter King Saul's camp. Everyone expected David to kill King Saul. Instead, David cut off a piece of Saul's skirt as Saul lay sleeping in a cave. The Bible then tells us:

> And it came to pass afterward, that David's heart smote him, because he had cut off Saul's skirt.
> —1 SAMUEL 24:5

David was being torn apart by his conscience for what he had done. (See 1 Samuel 24:6.) Do you know why David's conscience was giving him such a difficult time? It was because God had placed Saul as king. When God places a man as king, only God can remove him.

In 2 Samuel 24:10, we find David's conscience bothering him again. In an attempt to show Israel's strength to their enemies, pride prompted David to number the fighting men of Israel:

> And David's heart smote him after that he had numbered the people. And David said unto the LORD, I have sinned greatly in that I have done: and now, I beseech thee, O LORD, take away the iniquity of thy servant; for I have done very foolishly.

Do you recall in the Bible where God says David was a man after God's own heart? I believe the reason for this is

8

that David kept short accounts. As soon as David realized he was in sin, he got right with God. David asked for forgiveness and cleansing. He asked for restoration. David's heart smote him before he sinned and while he sinned. His heart then smote him after he sinned. We can learn a valuable lesson from how David lived before the Lord.

Have you ever had a time in your life when the devil would put a certain thing in front of you and say, "See what you did ten years ago?" You then cry out, "Oh, God, I'm sorry." You then find yourself praying for the same thing over and over again, not trusting that God has already forgiven you. Praying over and over again is a result of unbelief. You do not believe Jesus has cleansed you from all sin. Accept the truth; He has cleansed us from all sin. If you are feeling bad about a certain sin, repent and ask God to cleanse you in the precious blood of Jesus. Confess your sin to God. Do not allow the devil to torment you. God is not a man that He can lie, nor the son of man that He shall repent, nor turn His mind around or change His mind. (See Numbers 23:19.) God will forgive you. "If we confess our sins, he is faithful and just to forgive us our sins, and to cleanse us from all unrighteousness" (1 John 1:9). His arm is forever stretched out to you and me.

New Testament Teaching

The word *conscience* is used thirty-one times in the New Testament. In Mark 3:5 we find:

> And when he had looked round about on them with anger, being grieved for the hardness of their hearts, he saith unto the man, Stretch forth thine hand. And he stretched it out: and his hand was restored whole as the other.

9

Mark 3 tells us the Pharisees constantly watched Jesus in order to accuse Him of wrongdoing on the Sabbath. The Pharisees were a group that followed religious traditions rather than the truth of God's Word. Through the keeping of their own traditions, they had separated themselves from what was right and true according to God. Man's traditions will do this. In the verse above, it says Jesus was "grieved for the hardness of their hearts." The Pharisees' own traditions had caused them to be insensitive and callous to the truth. According to the Pharisees, healing could not take place on the Sabbath.

In that same verse, the Greek translation for "hardness of heart" is "hardness of conscience." The Pharisees had hardened their consciences to the point that they were seared. They were angry with Jesus because He was making waves. Because they had changed so much of the Word of God into tradition, they were no longer sensitive to God's truth. When you and I walk in the Word and in the light of the Word and are around people who are walking in religious tradition, we too will rock the boat. Jesus tells us that the Word is made void through tradition. (See Mark 7:13.)

Our conscience also lets us know that we are in right standing with the Lord. First John 3:19 says, "And hereby we know that we are of the truth, and shall assure our hearts before him." You are in right standing with the Lord if your conscience is not condemning you. I've had some people say, "I just do not know if it is sin or not." But they know. Their conscience tells them whether it is sin or not. Their conscience will speak to them, and it will always agree with the Word of God. One thing man did not lose in the Fall was his conscience. Much was lost when Adam sinned, but not his conscience.

10

Another area in which our conscience speaks to us is when we are talking or thinking about another person. Take a look at this next verse:

> Curse not the king, no not in thy thought; and curse not the rich in thy bedchamber: for a bird of the air shall carry the voice, and that which hath wings shall tell the matter.
>
> —ECCLESIASTES 10:20

If we say something about another person and we begin to hear our conscience, the best thing for us to do is to keep quiet. If we continue speaking and our conscience is telling us not to, we will break fellowship with that person. Because it is sin, we also will break fellowship with the Lord. The moment our conscience begins speaking to us that what we are saying or thinking is wrong, we should back up, ask forgiveness, and get away from it.

One important thing we need to remember is that our conscience does not take the place of the Holy Spirit. God uses our conscience to bring us into a life of being led by His Holy Spirit. There is a double government coming forth as God uses our conscience to lead us into being totally led by His Spirit. There will come a time when we are past the "No, do not do this," or "Be careful, come back" phase. We will come to a place where we begin hearing, "This is the way. Walk ye in it." Praise God. It is so easy to walk with the Lord once you begin to obey your conscience. Your conscience and the voice of the Lord work together. As you hear your conscience, the Lord's voice then comes forth and you have clear guidance. You learn how to walk in Spirit and truth first by obeying the conscience and secondly by Scripture.

11

THE WEAK CONSCIENCE

Possibly this is the first time you have read or even heard a teaching on the conscience from a biblical perspective. If you're wondering, (Does the Bible truly speak about the conscience?) then wonder no more. God's Word discusses the conscience throughout the New Testament. The next question we might ask is, (Why does the Bible speak so much about our conscience?) The reason is, God wants us to understand that the conscience is for our guidance and safety.

Our level of understanding and faith in God's Word determines whether we have a weak or strong conscience. In 1 Corinthians 8:7–12, Paul explains how eating meat offered to an idol can become a stumbling block to a Christian with a weak conscience:

> Howbeit there is not in every man that knowledge: for some with conscience of the idol unto this hour eat it as a thing offered unto an idol; and their conscience being weak is defiled.
>
> —1 CORINTHIANS 8:7

During the days Paul is speaking of, times were very hard, and some people would buy meat at what was called "the shambles." The shambles was a type of market that sold meat at a very cheap price. Idol worshipers there also sold the rest of an animal that had not been used as a sacrificial offering to their gods. Many times the idol worshipers would have a big feast and would cook and sell the meat. People were able to buy and eat the best meat in town for a very cheap price. In regard to our previous scripture, there were Christians who (before they became believers in Christ) had participated in idol worship. Because of their past involvement and their

12

lack of true understanding that idols were nothing, these Christians considered sacrifices offered to an idol as worship to a real and living god. Their conscience now being trained in Christianity told them this was wrong. For those who did not have full understanding or were weak in the faith, it was wrong for them to eat this meat because to them that idol represented much more than it did to someone who knew the idol was nothing. Even though they were Christians and no longer worshiped the idol, they had not yet come to the understanding that there is only one true God, that Christians do not become more or less spiritual by eating meat or any other food for that matter. Our acceptance before God or our approval from Him is not based on what we eat. (See 1 Corinthians 8:8.)

In verses 9 through 13 of 1 Corinthians 8, Paul goes on to explain how it is possible for a spiritually mature Christian to cause a Christian who is weak in faith and understanding to stumble and sin. Even though a spiritually mature Christian knows eating meat offered to a demon idol will not harm him, he should refrain from doing so when in the company of less mature Christians. The reason is that by following the example of a mature Christian, the one who is weak may go against the guidance of his conscience and decide to eat the meat anyway, knowing his conscience is telling him it is wrong to do so. A strong faith and full understanding of our freedom in Christ is not meant to cause another to stumble and sin. Not only is it a sin committed against a fellow Christian, the Bible tells us it is also a sin against Christ:

And through thy knowledge shall the weak brother perish, for whom Christ died? But when ye sin so against the brethren, and wound their weak conscience, ye sin against Christ. Wherefore, if meat make my brother to

13

offend, I will eat no flesh while the world standeth, lest
I make my brother to offend.

—1 CORINTHIANS 8:11–13

TRAINING YOUR CONSCIENCE

Our walk with the Lord should be one that is constantly growing and maturing unto all things. As we grow and mature in the Lord, the Holy Spirit trains, prompts, enlightens, and bears witness with our conscience to the point we are like a finely tuned instrument. Walking in the Spirit and spending time in God's Word and in prayer are the training grounds for fine-tuning the conscience. However, we must be careful to guard our conscience against religious tradition set in place by man. For example, there is a Christian group of people known as the Mennonites who love the Lord dearly. These people are somewhat similar to another group called the Amish. The Amish practice many traditions they believe help them spiritually. They are not allowed to drive cars but can use a horse and buggy to get around. They also wear the same type of clothing their great-grandparents wore when they came to America many years ago. These practices have been incorporated into their conscience in the name of religion.

Likewise, the Mennonites practice certain religious traditions they believe help them spiritually. To them it is a sin to be flashy. When they buy a car, they immediately paint all the chrome on it black. All of this, however, is what is known as adding to the gospel. Their conscience has been trained in error. What they believe to be right or wrong has been established by man, not by God.

There are areas in life in which we should heed what man has set in place. The difference here is that God guides and

14

influences what man sets in place. I am specifically referring to our civil authorities and the laws by which we are to abide. In Romans 13:1 we are told to be subject to the governing civil authorities because God has placed these people in positions of authority over us. In knowing this fact, Paul tells us we are to be subject not only to escape punishment, but also for the sake of our conscience: "Wherefore ye must needs be subject, not only for wrath, but also for conscience sake" (Rom. 13:5).

Training your conscience also requires listening to your conscience. Do not ignore it if it is convicting you of a certain matter. Listening to and obeying your conscience will bring you peace and joy. Nothing anyone says or does will convince you a certain matter is right or wrong if you have the witness of your conscience leading and guiding you. You simply cannot be moved.

> For our rejoicing is this, the testimony of our conscience, that in simplicity and godly sincerity, not with fleshly wisdom, but by the grace of God, we have had our conversation in the world, and more abundantly to you-ward.
>
> —2 CORINTHIANS 1:12

Many times Christians wonder if the Holy Spirit is speaking to them or not. Paul says in Romans 9:1 that our conscience lets us know whether the Holy Spirit is speaking to us or not: "I say the truth in Christ, I lie not, my conscience also bearing me witness in the Holy Ghost." The checks and balances God has given us to help our walk in the Spirit is the witness of both our conscience and the Holy Spirit. Christians are commanded to be spiritual and to do the things of the Spirit. But how will we know? We know by our conscience bearing

15

witness not only in God's Word, but also in the Holy Spirit. We are able to confirm what our conscience is saying by the testimony of God's Word and His Holy Spirit.

It is important for Christians to put the same emphasis on their conscience as God does. You would be surprised how this will draw you closer to the Lord. Listening to and obeying your conscience will keep you out of sin and help you keep your joy. You then begin to hear the Spirit say, "This is the way. Walk ye in it." Thank God for our conscience.

God, I thank You for being made in Your image. I thank You for giving me a conscience so that I might know right from wrong and good from evil. That knowing this, I can walk in truth. From this time on, I pray I will listen to my conscience, being Spirit-led, and have peace without torment. Help me to know my conscience will do a perfect work and that it is continually being restored in Christ. In Jesus' name I pray. Amen.

Chapter 2

OBEYING YOUR CONSCIENCE

WHEN MAN WAS created in the image and likeness of God, God also gave him a conscience. Some people say the human conscience is what separates man from beast. Even though some people have a seared conscience and are in sin, one thing is for sure. The Bible says their conscience still accuses or excuses them by letting them know right from wrong and good from evil.

We know the conscience works in three ways. It speaks to us before we sin, during the sin, and after the sin. The conscience continues its work until we are washed and cleansed in the blood of Jesus Christ. Once we confess and repent of our sin, the conscience miraculously leaves us alone. We are at peace when our conscience is at peace. Following the guidance our conscience provides is the primary step to being led by the Spirit. If we are unable to take the first step, how could it be possible to be led by God's Holy Spirit? It would not be possible.

Many people think the conscience functions in only a negative capacity, that it is always saying no to this or no to that. But there comes a time when the Holy Spirit begins using your conscience to guide and teach you. The conscience bears witness and is in agreement with God's Word and His Holy Spirit. It is important we understand that God has

17

given us a conscience to use for our growth, health, and to serve His kingdom.

SINCERITY AND WISDOM

Every Christian has a certain function in the body of Christ. In 2 Corinthians 1:12, Paul explains how he judges his own actions in regard to his ministry:

> [For our rejoicing is this, the testimony of our conscience, that in simplicity and godly sincerity, not with fleshly wisdom, but by the grace of God, we have had our conversation in the world, and more abundantly to you-ward.]

Throughout Paul's ministry, he was constantly accused, followed, and harassed by Judaizers. The Judaizers were a group of Jewish priests and scholars who tried to bring the church into the bondage of the Law. They believed a person could not be saved unless they kept the letter of the Law. Paul spoke against this view throughout his ministry. He worked hard to protect the church from this. In his effort to protect the church, Paul says in 2 Corinthians 1:12 that his conscience bears witness that he is walking the right path. His conscience tells him it is in the simplicity of the Word that we are saved through Christ Jesus.

God's Word declares we should never leave the simplicity of Christ Jesus. I have seen many churches get tired of the gospel. They begin adding and taking away from the simplicity of the gospel. Churches should not do this. They are to stay with the simplicity of Jesus Christ. A sign is placed on every pulpit in each of our churches that says, ["Preacher, preach Jesus Christ."] If for some reason we have to stop preaching Jesus, we will fight to continue preaching Jesus.

HAVE THE RIGHT MOTIVE

In 2 Corinthians 1:12 we also learn that having the right motive for our actions is important. Our actions and motives as Christians should not be influenced or guided by fleshly or earthly wisdom. Like Paul, our actions should spring from devout and pure motives with godly sincerity.

Notice in that same verse that Paul attributes the integrity and character of his motives to the Lord God. He recognizes his motives are guided by God and not by earthly wisdom. In the beginning of this verse, Paul says the testimony of his conscience gives support to his motives and conduct. This is something we all can learn from. If you are in doubt concerning your motives, search your conscience for the answer. It will guide you in the right path. Remember that the job of the conscience is to deal with you before, during, and after. Do not fool yourself into thinking that because you are chosen of God that all your motives are right. Always check your conscience to see if your motives are true to the Lord God and His ways.

Our conscience is the judgment seat we carry with us all the time. Use it—do not ignore it. God has linked our conscience to His moral will. We are ultimately responsible to God for listening to and obeying our conscience. If we do not take the first step in being led of God through obeying our conscience, how can we ever expect to be a Spirit-led Christian?

THE ORGAN OF KNOWING

The universal organ for knowing the moral and ethical will of God is man's conscience. The conscience always tells the truth. In Romans 2:11–16, Paul explains how our conscience works. It works not only for the saved but for the lost as well.

19

The conscience does not work as well in the lost because they lack Christian training. But their conscience does work. Let's take a look at what Paul says in Romans 2:11–16:

> For there is no respect of persons with God. For as many as have sinned without law shall also perish without law; and as many as have sinned in the law shall be judged by the law; (For not the hearers of the law are just before God, but the doers of the law shall be justified. For when the Gentiles, which have not the law, do by nature the things contained in the law, these, having not the law, are a law unto themselves: Which shew the work of the law written in their hearts, their conscience also bearing witness, and their thoughts the mean while accusing or else excusing one another;) In the day when God shall judge the secrets of men by Jesus Christ according to my gospel.

In the verses above we see God has placed in all men the ability to know right from wrong. Man's conscience bears witness to the moral and ethical will of God. Our morals are what guide us in what is right and wrong in our conduct. Ethics are the moral code or moral standard of our conduct. Ethics bring you to morals, character, and integrity. Medical doctors are supposed to have ethical standards—how much more the church? Some say, "Well, that's all right because we are free in Christ." We must remember the conscience always lifts us to the truth. It causes us to be conscious of God's right and wrong, and of good and evil. The conscience will compare our deeds, words, and thoughts with the will and Word of God.

20

YOUR MINISTRY WITH JESUS

How many times have you asked yourself if what you were doing in your ministry was the right thing? At the same time you are questioning yourself, it seems the enemy comes along and tries to beat you down. In Acts 23:1 we find Paul being condemned for his ministry with Jesus. His reply was, "And Paul, earnestly beholding the council, said, Men and brethren, I have lived in all good conscience before God until this day." Do you think there is anyone today who can say the same thing as Paul did? Some may think Paul must have been an extra good saint to be able to say he lived with a good conscience before God. I believe Paul was completely committed to the Lord and his ministry. When Paul found the truth, he married the truth. He became one with Christ in every aspect of his life, including his thinking. Some Christians believe they are in Christ, yet there is a part of their life they hold back for themselves. The Bible tells us, "For ye are bought with a price: therefore glorify God in your body, and in your spirit, which are God's" (1 Cor. 6:20).

To see if there is an area in your life that you are holding on to, check yourself on the following question. Have you ever thought about your past and said, "I wish I hadn't done that"? If you have, let it go and remember this: the blood of Christ cleanses you from all sin. "For this is thankworthy, if a man for conscience toward God endure grief, suffering wrongfully" (1 Pet. 2:19). Keep this verse in remembrance if for some reason you have been treated badly, picked on at work, unjustly accused of something, or whatever the reason. The Bible tells us even when we know we have done right and yet suffer wrongfully, there will be a day when the Lord will set all things right. "Vengeance is mine saith the Lord. I will repay" (Heb. 10:30.) Let the Lord have that thing. Do

21

not carry it around with you. If you do not, you will begin to violate your conscience because you will want to retaliate. Instead, give it to the Lord and be Spirit-led.

It seems in this day and time, it is a lost art to suffer wrongfully but keep still about it. There are those who are consumed with repaying the ones that have caused them to suffer wrongfully. But this in itself is wrong. The moment we find our conscience speaking to us when we are suffering wrongfully, we should stop and obey. When we humble ourselves before the Lord, He will lift us up.

An important lesson we can learn from 1 Peter 2:19 is that even though people may accuse us of being wrong, our conscience will step in and let us know we are right in a certain matter. We can trust our conscience in all circumstances. We have seen from earlier Scripture passages that God has made it so that even the lost know right from wrong:

> For when the Gentiles, which have not the law, do by nature the things contained in the law, these, having not the law, are a law unto themselves: Which shew the work of the law written in their hearts, their conscience also bearing witness, and their thoughts the mean while accusing or else excusing one another.
> —ROMANS 2:14–15

For those that are lost and do not have Jesus Christ as their Savior, Romans 2:14–15 will speak to their conscience. Their conscience will say, "Amen. That's true." They know they have sinned and come short. They know the soul within them shall die. They are under conviction and eternal death. If the lost person listens to his conscience in the next verse, he will know he can be justified freely by God's grace through redemption in Christ Jesus:

22

For all have sinned, and come short of the glory of God; Being justified freely by his grace through the redemption that is in Christ Jesus.

—ROMANS 3:23–24

Some people have told me they do not believe in Jesus Christ as a Savior. If they were to listen to their conscience, they would get an "amen" on that, too. Our conscience verifies the total Word of God. It knows that God has set forth Jesus to be a propitiation through faith in His blood.

One thing I have noticed that some mainline churches do is back away from singing songs about the blood of Jesus. If you were to check their songbooks, you would not find many (if any) songs about the blood of Jesus. If the leaders of these churches were to check their consciences, they would find that only the blood of Jesus will wash away sins. They would find that their consciences agree with the Word and the Holy Spirit.

Whom God hath set forth to be a propitiation through faith in his blood, to declare his righteousness for the remission of sins that are past, through the forbearance of God; To declare, I say, at this time his righteousness: that he might be just, and the justifier of him which believeth in Jesus. Where is boasting then? It is excluded. By what law? of works? Nay: but by the law of faith. Therefore we conclude that a man is justified by faith without the deeds of the law.

—ROMANS 3:25–28

LIVING BY FAITH AND NOT WORKS

Some Christians work hard at trying to keep themselves saved. But the Bible tells us we are saved by faith, not works. (See Romans 3:28.) When we receive Christ Jesus as Lord, we

23

are to walk in all that He has provided for us, living by faith in His finished work at the cross. We are to have faith that we were crucified with Christ, buried with Him, and raised with newness of life. Our faith is to grab hold of the promise that if any man be in Christ, he is a new creature. Old things have passed away. All things are made new and are of God. Our life is now hidden with Christ in God.

It is a lie from the devil if we think we have to keep ourselves saved. Because we are too busy taking care of ourselves and not realizing the totality of our salvation, God is not able to use us in greater things. We are too preoccupied with ourselves to be used by God. It is important to understand and have faith in God's Word. He says we are a new creation, we are in His kingdom, we are now in Christ and accepted in our beloved Lord.

Our conscience testifies to these blessed truths. The problem is, some Christians do not listen to their consciences about these blessings and as a result their life is one big yo-yo. They wonder, "Where is the Spirit of God? I'm supposed to be in the Spirit. I'm supposed to have gifts and a ministry. Where are these things?"

One thing is for sure, the Holy Spirit respects your conscience, no matter what shape it's in. Romans 9:1 tells us, "I say the truth in Christ, I lie not, my conscience also bearing me witness in the Holy Ghost." When you and I do not respect our conscience, it is the same as saying, "I will not be Spirit-led."

There are two ways our conscience witnesses in the Holy Spirit. Some people are afraid of getting some other type of spirit. They are the ones who are afraid of coming into the baptism of the Holy Spirit because they think (for example,) a snake will get them instead of the Holy Spirit. But your conscience tells you whether it is the Holy Spirit or not and is the first way our conscience witnesses in the Holy Spirit. Secondly, the Holy Spirit witnesses *to* our conscience. When we ignore our conscience we have an unstable walk with the Lord because we are ignoring His Holy Spirit.

My Testimony

I received the baptism of the Holy Spirit in 1958. It was during the time when people were being thrown out of their churches for receiving the Holy Spirit. Likewise I was thrown out of child evangelism for receiving the baptism of the Holy Spirit. At that time I was director of San Diego County and worked with some eighty or more teachers. They kept their doctrine pure, but there were problems later on. Anyway, we had revival going on. More than one hundred children per month were being saved. I am talking about first decisions made for the Lord, not second, third, or fourth decisions that kids make. During this time I went to different churches trying to be grounded in the things of the Spirit. But something inside me would tell me "this is wrong" and "that is wrong." I knew it was not the devil telling me these things because I knew God's Word then as I do now. I found that my spirit was keeping me on the Word.

I say the truth in Christ. My conscience also bears my witness in the Holy Spirit. When you begin to trust your conscience, you will know, too. You will not be saying, "I wish I knew if this were God, or me, or the devil." Begin obeying your conscience now. Your conscience will always bring you to the Holy Spirit and the Word of God.

When a person is in sin, his conscience convicts him. We can see this plainly in John 8:3–9:

> And the scribes and Pharisees brought unto him a woman taken in adultery; and when they had set her

25

in the midst, They say unto him, Master, this woman was taken in adultery, in the very act. Now Moses in the law commanded us, that such should be stoned: but what sayest thou? This they said, tempting him, that they might have to accuse him. But Jesus stooped down, and with his finger wrote on the ground, as though he heard them not. So when they continued asking him, he lifted up himself, and said unto them, He that is without sin among you, let him first cast a stone at her. And again he stooped down, and wrote on the ground. And they which heard it, being convicted by their own conscience, went out one by one, beginning at the eldest, even unto the last: and Jesus was left alone, and the woman standing in the midst.

In the verses above, we see the accusers being convicted by their own consciences. One by one they all left. Jesus was left alone with the woman. If you are in sin today, your conscience will tell you. You should say yes to your conscience and get right with God. God wants you to have a life of joy. Ignoring your conscience will rob your life of joy. Ignoring your conscience is the same as ignoring the Holy Spirit and the written Word of God.

How does God want us to live?

And herein do I exercise myself, to have always a conscience void of offence toward God, and toward men.

—ACTS 24:16

Lord, I pray for sincerity and wisdom of the conscience. That I would exercise myself to have a conscience void of offense toward You and toward man. In Jesus' name. Amen.

26

Chapter 3

THE REVELATION OF THE CONSCIENCE

WHERE WOULD THE church be today if Luther had not cared about conscience? In boldness Luther declared, "It is neither right nor safe to go against my conscience."[1] What a tremendous testimony. God had revealed to Luther not only the truth of salvation through faith but also the truth about man's conscience. Luther trusted his conscience to the point he based his whole ministry on it. Yet today it seems there are Spirit-filled Christians who have battered their conscience so much they can hardly hear it. The difference between Luther and other people could very well be in the way the conscience is treated. Having a ministry or not may be in the way a person treats their conscience.

The Word of God tells us in Proverbs 20:27, "The spirit of man is the candle of the LORD, searching all the inward parts of the belly." The Moffatt translation of this verse says, "Man's conscience is the lamp of the Eternal flashing into his inner most soul."[2] We know the conscience tells us when we are right or wrong. I believe it speaks louder when we are right than when we are wrong.

27

RELYING ON YOUR CONSCIENCE

It seems that many people have only a negative conscience, or rather they only listen when it's saying "this is wrong." But it is possible for us to trust the conscience when it says "this is right." Listening to only one side of the conscience is like an engine running on only half of its cylinders. The engine will move you, but only at half the speed.

During counseling sessions I have had people ask me, "Should I buy this or that?" or "Is this too much or too little to pay?" I am able to give them a fast, sure word out of my conscience. By the Spirit of the Lord, I can tell them just about every time the exact money they will pay. God lets them know what they can get it for. Our finances is just one of the areas in which He wants us all to be Spirit-led.

We know our conscience tells us right from wrong, but what else does it tell us? It also lets us know when something is good or evil. If something is good, do you bother to check it out? Most magazines seem to look good on the cover, but that in itself does not really tell you anything until you open it and investigate what's inside. Once you check inside you may find it is rotten. The point is, check it out.

Has your conscience ever warned you that you were about to slip into something evil? Many times people wait until they have one foot in the evil before they actually say anything about it. The world has a word for this type of warning. With men it's a *hunch*, and with women it's their *intuition*. Wouldn't it be wonderful to have a blood-washed, Spirit-led conscience?

28

GOD-GIVEN SELF-DETERMINATION

Do you know where your conscience is located in your body? It is in your heart. God has also given us self-determination in that we are free to give ourselves to Him. Your conscience will help guide you in giving yourself to the Lord. If a religious spirit came along while you were giving yourself to the Lord and you were not able to discern the spirit, your conscience would guide you right past it. It would tell you right from wrong and good from evil.

> Let us draw near with a true heart in full assurance of faith, having our hearts sprinkled from an evil conscience, and our bodies washed with pure water.
> —HEBREWS 10:22

THE CONSCIENCE REVEALS

So far we have seen how God uses man's conscience to guide him. The conscience functions on morals—knowing what is right and wrong. Because God has given man a conscience, his conscience reflects the will of God all the time. Learning the ethical will of God allows man's conscience to work at its best. Knowing that the conscience makes its home in the heart of man, it is easy to understand the importance of giving ourselves to the Lord. When we have given ourselves to Him, He cleanses our heart. The Lord cleanses us. Praise God for His Son.

Did you know each time you read the Word your conscience grabs on to it and memorizes it immediately? This is one reason why it is so important to be in a church that has a lot of good teaching on the Word.

Have you ever noticed how you react when your conscience is bothering you? What happens when your conscience bothers you? For one thing, there is no rest. You lose your peace. There is no stability in your walk with the Lord. (Have you ever noticed that you feel oppressed when your conscience is bothering you?)

Earlier we saw how David's conscience was at work when he cut a small portion off of Saul's skirt (1 Sam. 24:5) and when he numbered Israel (2 Sam. 24:10). The Bible says his heart smote him; his conscience told him what he had done was wrong. This is a clear example of your conscience working against you.

THE HEART REACTS

The Bible says we are made in the image and likeness of God. Point by point, we are made like God. Point by point, He is able to fill us with His life. Every part of you is a vessel for the life of Christ so that His life may be manifested in you. (How does our conscience fit in with all of this? Would our lives be any different if we were to listen to our conscience? How many times have we said, "I hope I'm doing the right thing"?) When we allow the Lord to fill us with Himself, only then will we know we are on the right path. What a wonderful rest to know we are doing the right thing instead of wondering all the time. (How can we claim to be sons of God if we walk in doubt all the time?) When we begin obeying our conscience, we will continue to grow spiritually.

(Have you ever done something against your conscience?) Maybe it was something your conscience got a hold of you about and you decided to push aside the advice of your conscience. Knowing the entire time that you were wrong, you still did not heed what your conscience was telling you. Take a look at the next verse:

[For when the Gentiles, which have not the law, do by nature the things contained in the law, these, having not the law, are a law unto themselves: Which shew the work of the law written in their hearts, their conscience also bearing witness, and their thoughts the mean while accusing or else excusing one another.]

—ROMANS 2:14–15

Our conscience works in our heart and thoughts. Even the lost know right from wrong. The Lord holds them guilty when they disobey the leading of their conscience. If instead they were to follow their conscience, they would walk pleasingly unto the Lord.

God always saves those who seek Him. Cornelius is an example of this in the New Testament. How do you suppose Moses's father-in-law became a priest before he knew anything about Moses? God has always had a people, a remnant. God uses man's conscience to witness to the saved and unsaved alike.

HEARING THE HOLY SPIRIT

Many times Christians will say, "I get a witness." Those who have learned to listen to their conscience will always hear the Holy Spirit. My conscience also bears "me witness in the Holy Ghost" (Rom. 9:1). Those who do not will never learn to listen to the Holy Spirit because the Holy Spirit uses the conscience. How can we check our inner voice to determine if the Holy Spirit is talking to us or not?

When the apostle Paul spoke God's Word, he would test it by the Holy Spirit and his conscience. When Paul received a word from the Lord, he did not begin running off at the mouth. Instead, he checked that word to make

31

sure it was from the Lord. He used his conscience to do the checking—the part of him that told him right from wrong and good from evil. Our conscience always lets us know if it is God speaking or not. When we take the first step in obeying our conscience, we grow continuously in the Spirit of the Lord.

CHECKING YOUR WALK WITH THE LORD

Have you ever wanted to check your walk to make sure all is right with the Lord? Some people ask for counsel when their conscience has already given them an answer. The answer they receive in counsel many times confirms what their conscience already was saying. Confirmation is good when it is received. Christians have a built-in word unless they try to compromise that word. We should not argue with our conscience, but instead we should trust it like the Word.

THE RELIGIOUS SPIRIT

When Christians listen to a religious spirit rather than their conscience, problems occur with their walk with the Lord. Sometimes a religious spirit will convince a person to endure suffering when this was not the Lord's plan at all. This happened to me one time. That religious spirit moved me off base and my whole family suffered because of it. Even though my conscience was screaming the whole time, "Do not do this," I decided to do this thing because I felt it was right. I was going to suffer, and I was willing to suffer for the Lord. But it was a religious spirit causing the suffering and not the Lord.

You may ask, "Where was your discernment?" It was working hand-in-hand with the leading of my conscience.

Sometimes sincere Christians turn their backs on their conscience and go through tremendous suffering, all in the name of the Lord. There are times the Lord will lead us in suffering. We are commanded to go into suffering and we will have suffering. If we suffer with Him we will also rule with Him.

Our conscience will guide us if we listen. If it says suffering is right, then we should suffer. One thing we should be careful of is when a friend has discernment and yet begins to pity us for our suffering. Their conscience will witness to them that your suffering is in line with the Lord, but because of pity they will ignore their conscience. In the New Testament, Peter told the Lord, "O Lord pity thyself. Don't go to the cross" (Matt. 15:22, GENEVA). Peter was not listening to his conscience. "For this is thankworthy, if a man for conscience toward God endure grief, suffering wrongfully" (1 Pet. 2:19).

It seems the art of suffering is rare these days. No one likes to suffer. However, our conscience will guide us and let us know if we are really in the way of the Lord or not.

THE PROCESS OF PERCEPTION

What does *conscience* mean? It means to arouse from death, to revive and restore to life. It means co-perception. The word *co* in the Greek is a prefix meaning "an association or accompanying action." It means someone is helping someone else along. Our conscience is an inner witness walking along with us. If you have a problem, talk it over with your conscience. It will help you solve the problem.

Perception is a process of knowing moral value. It is an active process of knowing, seeing, and understanding. Perception causes you to be aware and informed. All of these descriptions point to a Christian who is filled with the Holy Spirit. A Christian who listens to the leading of the Holy Spirit in his or her conscience is one who has keen perception.

LIVING IN GOOD CONSCIENCE

The Bible says in Acts 23:1, "And Paul, earnestly beholding the council, said, Men and brethren, I have lived in all good conscience before God until this day." Why didn't Paul say he was Spirit-led in his living before the Lord? The men he was talking to would not have understood what that meant. They did not have the Spirit, but each of them had a conscience. When a man stands up and says he has never violated his conscience, he is either a liar or a very godly man. Each Christian should live a life in all good conscience and be able to say what Paul said in this verse.

Your conscience and God's Word are aligned as one and say the same word. Your conscience will never say anything contrary to the Word of God. Martin Luther realized his conscience was bound to the Word, and he spoke publicly about it. There were people who wanted Luther to recall all his writings and sermons. They wanted him to renounce the truth he was preaching. But Luther said he could not. He told them, "My conscience is bound to the Word of God. I am not able to recall, nor do I wish to recall anything for it is neither faith, nor honest to do anything against the conscience. Here I stand. I cannot do otherwise. God help me."[3]

Luther was a man ready to die for the sake of not going against his conscience. No doubt there were people who tried to talk him out of his stand. But you know, none of us will be strong Christians if we violate our conscience. We will end

34

up being shifty, compromising, and always slipping around. We will never be steadfast, stable, or a true minister of God if we violate our conscience.

Lord, help me to not violate my God-given conscience. Help me to realize my conscience is bound to Your Word. As I obey my conscience, I obey Your Word, whether I have heard Your Word or not. In Jesus' name. Amen.

Chapter 4

THE CLEANSING OF THE CONSCIENCE

As far as Martin Luther was concerned, the entire Reformation stood upon man's conscience. This same attitude about the importance of the conscience has also been witnessed in the apostle Paul. Paul said that in Christ, he had never gone against his conscience. The conscience is such a major doctrine in the New Testament that it is a wonder more messages are not preached on it.

We know God made man in His image and likeness and that He gave man a conscience. The conscience guides and helps man monitor what is good and evil and what is right and wrong. Even the lost are accountable for going against their conscience because God has blessed them with knowing right from wrong and good from evil.

LINKED TO THE ETHICAL WILL OF GOD

The conscience is linked to the ethical will of God. He is a Gentleman, one who has character and ethics. When we have learned to obey our conscience, we will have a much better spiritual walk. Our paths will be straight. The more we learn to obey our conscience, the more we will be obeying the Holy Spirit. Because our conscience is a link to the ethical will of God, behind our conscience stands the authority of

God Himself, so much so that if we violate our conscience through disobedience, we will not be in right standing with the Lord. Violating the conscience causes a person to lose fellowship with God.

In Hebrews the Bible talks about washing the conscience in the blood of Jesus. People who are not governed by their consciences are in need of cleansing by the blood of Jesus. When a person is washed in the blood, his or her conscience is washed, too. Once a person is saved, all guilt flies away. It is a miracle in itself. Once the conscience is cleansed, it settles down and says yes to God. The Christian life becomes tied to God's will through the conscience. No longer can we say, "I didn't know," because through the conscience, the Holy Spirit guides and teaches us.

CLEANSING THE CONSCIENCE

I believe the verses in Jeremiah 31:31–33 are linked to the cleansing of the conscience, the blood-washing of the conscience, and the laws of God in the heart of man:

> Behold, the days come, saith the LORD, that I will make a new covenant with the house of Israel, and with the house of Judah: Not according to the covenant that I made with their fathers in the day that I took them by the hand to bring them out of the land of Egypt; which my covenant they brake, although I was an husband unto them, saith the LORD: But this shall be the covenant that I will make with the house of Israel; After those days, saith the LORD, I will put my law in their inward parts, and write it in their hearts; and will be their God, and they shall be my people.

From the moment a person is born again he knows inside what God wants and does not want. Sometimes people may ask you to pray for something that goes against your conscience. My advice is do not do it. This has happened to me. A group of people in a certain church were praying for a young girl. Time after time the girl would go to the altar. I had been visiting the church and was getting ready to leave when they asked me to see if God had a word. The people who were praying did not know what was bothering the girl. She wept at the altar all the time. As we began to pray for her, she stood in the middle of us and cried, not saying a word. Finally I said, "Thus saith the Lord: You want to marry a man who is not a Christian, and you are asking God for permission. You know it's wrong and He won't let you marry this man." The girl then replied, "That's a lie!" I told them that was the word I had received from the Lord, and then I began to walk out of the church to my car. The assistant pastor ran to catch up with me and said, "I'm the only one who knows it. Every word you said was the truth."

What had happened with the girl was her conscience was bothering her. She had been trying to get God to change His Word and He would not do it. After I left she eventually confessed to the group that she had lied. As far as I know she did not marry that lost man. She had been trying to go against her conscience, and she was so tender that it was tearing her up. Praise God! It saved her a lifetime of problems.

> I will put my law in their inward parts, and write it in their hearts; and will be their God, and they shall be my people.
>
> —JEREMIAH 31:33

39

ALL WERE CREATED WITH A CONSCIENCE

Jesus said in Matthew 7:11, "If ye then, being evil, know how to give good gifts unto your children, how much more shall your Father which is in heaven give good things to them that ask him?" Jesus is saying that people without salvation know good from evil and right from wrong. This knowledge was put in man at Creation; however, some Christians do not understand this and are full of excuses for their behavior. When the Word speaks to us about sin in our life, we must cleanse our conscience and begin fine-tuning it so that we may be right with God. This in turn causes the conscience to become more and more alive to the Holy Spirit.

Have you ever heard a phone ringing on a television program and wondered if it was your phone? Some Christians have treated their conscience in this manner. Their conscience has been violated to the point they cannot hear it ringing. They know they heard something, but they cannot tell where it is coming from.

Tuning out the conscience is a very dangerous thing. Some who do this wonder why they no longer have fellowship with the Lord. The reason is, the conscience has been violated. We must get right with the Lord and be cleansed so that we can enjoy His fellowship. God put the conscience in man before salvation so that all could come to Him. The Lord uses the conscience and the convicting power of the Holy Spirit to draw man unto Himself. God and His Holy Spirit work with your conscience.

FOLLOWING YOUR CONSCIENCE

The conscience is the inward part of man—the organ that reveals God's moral truth to man. When we follow our conscience we are lifted up to God. Not violating the conscience causes the Holy Spirit to use us and lift us up to a God-consciousness. If we violate the conscience, we are in sin and the door of fellowship with the Lord is closed until we confess, ask for forgiveness, and repent. In James 4:17, Jesus said, "Therefore to him that knoweth to do good, and doeth it not, to him it is sin." The Bible also says that when someone thinks about committing adultery, it is the same as if he or she had committed adultery. Here we see the conscience also monitoring our thought life.

When God mentions a certain subject more than thirty times in the Bible, it should be a major doctrine. Most preachers leave the subject of the conscience alone. We should not run from something we are not comfortable with—we should run to it. Thank God we have truth and that we can walk into the holy place just by staying out of sin.

> For there is no respect of persons with God. For as many as have sinned without law shall also perish without law: and as many as have sinned in the law shall be judged by the law; (For not the hearers of the law are just before God, but the doers of the law shall be justified. For when the Gentiles, which have not the law, do by nature the things contained in the law, these, having not the law, are a law unto themselves: Which shew the work of the law written in their hearts, their conscience also bearing witness, and their thoughts the mean while accusing or else excusing one another;) In the day when God shall judge the secrets of men by Jesus Christ according to my gospel.
>
> —ROMANS 2:11–16

One of the messages in this verse is that our conscience will tell us the same thing again and again. It does not waver.

If it is wrong today, it will be wrong tomorrow. If this is the way today, it will be the way tomorrow. Once we decide to obey the conscience in our walk with God, it becomes a positive and guiding voice by the Holy Spirit. Some people have asked me, "How do you know the will of the Lord so fast?" Simply because I have come to the positive side of my conscience. The conscience is a tremendous guide for leading you into the Holy Spirit.

BEARING WITNESS

The apostle Paul said his conscience bears witness in the Holy Spirit. (See Romans 9:1.) The conscience was a major doctrine in Paul's life. He knew the Holy Spirit and the will of God by his conscience. Anytime you and I are led by a spirit to violate our conscience, this leading is not by the Holy Spirit. A day will come when each person on Earth is judged according to his or her conscience. Paul says in Romans 2:15:

> Which shew the work of the law written in their hearts, their conscience also bearing witness, and their thoughts the mean while accusing or else excusing one another.

In our lifetime we have seen generation after generation throw their conscience away. We have seen it from the fifties through the nineties to today. I believe there are probably Christians who fool around with dope and other sorts of things. But they do not do these things with a clear conscience before God. Christians are not here on Earth to experiment with sin. We are here to do the will of God. We should let Acts 23:1 be a law in our lives: "And Paul, earnestly beholding the council, said, Men and brethren, I have lived in all good conscience before God until this day." I do not know of a stronger statement anywhere in the Word that someone could stand up and say. "Since I've known Christ, I have not violated my conscience." What a tremendous statement. No wonder God could use Paul.

HAVING A DOUBLE WITNESS

Living before God in good conscience shows that your conscience and God are linked closely. The knowledge you have of the will of God shows you the life you must live in good conscience before Him. Depending on the life you are living, God will either lift you up or put you under conviction. If you are in rebellion against God and His Word, your conscience remains faithful in talking to you and trying to steer you back to God.

The job of the conscience does not take away from the Holy Spirit's work in each of us. We have a double witness with the Spirit of God and our conscience both talking to and guiding us. The Holy Spirit says, "This is the way, walk ye in it," while your conscience says, "Yes, go." This is the double witness each Christian has when they obey their conscience.

CHANGING YOUR CONVERSATION

In 1 Peter 2:9–19 we find more evidence for keeping our conscience pure before God:

> But ye are a chosen generation, a royal priesthood, an holy nation, a peculiar people; that ye should show forth the praises of him who hath called you out of darkness into his marvellous light. Which in time past were not a people, but are now the people of God: which had not obtained mercy, but now have obtained mercy. Dearly beloved, I beseech you as strangers and pilgrims.
> —1 PETER 2:9–11

43

The people spoken to in the previous verses are newborn Christians who now have the responsibility of learning a new way of life and learning about their conscience, "abstain from fleshly lusts, which war against the soul." They are now expected to live according to their conscience.

Having your conversation honest among the Gentiles: that whereas they speak against you as evildoers, they may by your good works, which they shall behold, glorify God in the day of visitation. Submit yourselves to every ordinance of man for the Lord's sake: whether it be to the king, as supreme. Or unto governor, as unto them that are sent by him for the punishment of evildoers, and for the praise of them that do well. For so is the will of God, that with well doing ye may put to silence the ignorance of foolish men. As free, and not using your liberty for a cloak of maliciousness, but as servants of God. Honour all men. Love the brotherhood. Fear God. Honour the king. Servants, be subject to your masters with all fear; not only to the good and gentle, but also to the froward. For this is thanksworthy, if a man for conscience toward God endure grief, suffering wrongfully.

—1 PETER 2:12–19

We see that the verses above are all about the conscience. Someone might ask, What if I'm innocent and someone is walking all over me? The verses say we are to stay in good conscience and not sin.

We are to keep our conscience pure before God so that we can serve Him. Sometimes when a person pushes us around we want to retaliate. We end up getting in the flesh about it and getting into sin. At this point God cannot use us because we are no better than the one who is causing us problems. The

Bible says we are to stay in good conscience before God. This places our conscience in the will of the Lord. We no longer have a yo-yo life—up one day, down the next. Instead, our life has guidance through our conscience knowing God's will.

> *Lord, please forgive me and cleanse me that I may keep a good conscience before You and toward man. Forgive me and cleanse me by washing me in the precious blood of Christ. May I from this day forward obey my conscience and keep it pleasing unto You. Even during grief, I want to keep myself clean and pure before You for Your service. In Jesus' name. Amen.*

Chapter 5

THE SECRET AUTHORITY

MANY PEOPLE SAY, "I don't know the will of the Lord. I wish I knew." God has built within each person the ability to know His will. We are told in God's Word that people who do not know or read the Bible still know His will. When God created man in His image and likeness, He placed within man the very morals that He has. The Lord created each of us with a conscience that acts as our secret authority knowing right from wrong and good from evil.

THE LIGHT OF THE CONSCIENCE

Man's conscience is the secret authority inside himself that monitors his thoughts, actions, and words. The Lord's moral standards serve as a light to the conscience in such a way that man is aware of what God expects of him. God's moral standards are linked to man's conscience, allowing him to know right from wrong and good from evil, regardless if he is saved or not.

STEPPING INTO SIN

When we step into sin it is as if we push the guidance of our conscience and the Holy Spirit to one side. God created man in such a way that His moral convictions are fixed inside man. Man's conscience will always trouble him when he goes against his conscience. Even if he is raised in a way that teaches him to do certain things that are against God's moral standards, his conscience will still trouble him.

In previous chapters we discovered what the Bible says about man's conscience. Great men of God such as the apostle Paul and Martin Luther understood the blessed truths God has provided in His Word about man's conscience. Both of these men surrendered completely to the guiding light of their consciences and the Holy Spirit.

Martin Luther was a Catholic priest used of God during the Reformation. Luther's desire was to see the Catholic Church return to the ways of God. He wanted the church to get back to the simplicity of the gospel, preaching the good news of Jesus Christ. At the time there were those who opposed Luther in his desire for the church. These men commanded Luther to recall and renounce the message he preached and wrote about. Luther was making waves in the church. This will happen when we come against religious traditions set up by man in the church.

When we obey our conscience as Luther did, both the Word of God and the Holy Spirit witness to our conscience. Our conscience does not walk in confusion when the Holy Spirit and God's Word confirm and support what the conscience is saying to us. We have the assurance that we are right in what we say, do, or think. This is what Luther meant when he said, "Here I stand. I cannot do otherwise."[1] Luther knew he was right in what he desired for the church because of the witness of his conscience.

CONSCIENCE SUPPLIES LIGHT AND TRUTH

What happens when we disobey our conscience? Let's take a look at Genesis 3:8–10 and see how Adam and Eve acted when they disobeyed their consciences:

> And they heard the voice of the LORD God walking in the garden in the cool of the day: and Adam and his wife hid themselves from the presence of the LORD God amongst the trees of the garden. And the LORD God called unto Adam, and said unto him, Where art thou? And he said, I heard thy voice in the garden, and I was afraid, because I was naked; and I hid myself.

Disobeying your conscience causes you to hide yourself from the presence of the Lord just as Adam and Eve did. In Hebrew, *I was afraid* translates as "my heart smote me" (1 John 1:4–9, author's paraphrase). Adam's heart had convicted him of his sin. Because he knew he had disobeyed God, he hid himself from the presence of the Lord.

LET GOD BE GOD

Sometimes people become jealous of each other in the church. Their jealousy causes conflict within the church. There are those who believe they would make a better preacher, teacher, or evangelist than the one God has put in place. This is a dangerous attitude to have because God's anointing is on the one He has put in that position. It is up to the Lord to remove or set in place whom He wants—not man. We are not to lay a hand upon God's anointed. David realized this truth when he cut off King Saul's skirt. The Bible tells us David's heart smote him for what he had done. Because of his conscience, he knew he had sinned against God.

> And it came to pass afterward, that David's heart smote him, because he had cut off Saul's skirt. And he said unto his men, The LORD forbid that I should do this thing unto my master, the LORD's anointed, to stretch forth mine hand against him, seeing he is the anointed of the LORD.
>
> —1 SAMUEL 24:5–6

In the Old Testament men and women of God walked in truth by the power of their conscience. The Holy Spirit would come upon them, but not as often as in the New Testament. It was God's plan to send His Holy Spirit to man after His Son, Jesus, was raised from the dead and sitting in heaven at His right hand. Because of Jesus, you and I are able to walk in the power of His Holy Spirit and in the power of our conscience.

God has equipped us well, but there are still those who say, "Well, I don't know the voice of the Spirit." Or, they say, "I just don't understand what the Spirit is saying." These people have overruled their consciences to the point that their heart has been hardened. The Bible speaks about assuring your heart to prove truth:

> For when the Gentiles, which have not the law, do by nature the things contained in the law, these, having not the law, are a law unto themselves: Which shew the work of the law written in their hearts, their conscience also bearing witness, and their thoughts the mean while accusing or else excusing one another;) In the day when God shall judge the secrets of men by Jesus Christ according to my gospel.
>
> —ROMANS 2:14–16

The verses above describe how these people will be judged based on whether they obeyed their conscience or not. When the Lord said in Genesis, "Let us make man in our image, after our likeness" (Gen. 1:26), He was saying "in our image" is Spirit, and "after our likeness" is a concrete example. "Morally the same" is what is meant by the words *concrete example.* In order for man to be morally the same as God, there had to be an absolute, built-in rule provided for man by God. That built-in rule took the form of the conscience—the light that illuminates every man who comes into the world.

We no longer have any reason to stand before God and say, "I didn't know." We are made in His image and likeness. He is our concrete example. We have been restored in Christ. We have been washed in the blood of Jesus. According to the book of Hebrews we have been renewed to perfection. All of this includes our conscience.

> For our rejoicing is this, the testimony of our conscience, that in simplicity and godly sincerity, not with fleshly wisdom, but by the grace of God, we had our conversation in the world, and more abundantly to you-ward.
> —2 Corinthians 1:12

WALKING ACCORDING TO CONSCIENCE

In the New Testament, foot-washing is mentioned one or two times. In some churches this is all they talk about. The water baptism is mentioned two or three times, and it seems that is all some churches talk about, too. However, the conscience is mentioned more than thirty times and you never hear it being taught. Teaching on the conscience touches everyone. When we ask for guidance from God, the first thing God expects is for us to obey our conscience. Why would the

Lord give us spiritual guidance if we violate our conscience through disobedience? To receive guidance from the Holy Spirit we first must do what we know to do: "Therefore to him that knoweth to do good, and doeth it not, to him it is sin" (James 4:17). If we want guidance from the Lord, the first thing we should do is walk according to our conscience. The next step will come by the voice of the Holy Spirit.

There are some people who do not agree with the baptism of the Holy Spirit. They believe in their hearts and consciences that the baptism of the Holy Spirit is forever passed away.

> Now the Spirit speaketh expressly, that in the latter times some shall depart from the faith, giving heed to seducing spirits, and doctrines of devils; Speaking lies in hypocrisy; having their conscience seared with a hot iron.
>
> —1 TIMOTHY 4:1–2

To speak a lie in hypocrisy means to speak something or receive something that is false as though it were truth. If I were to tell you a lie and you accepted it as truth, your conscience would be seared. It would become dead. The only way to take away the searing of the conscience is by the Word of God.

One time when I was a Baptist preacher, I had decided to speak a series of messages against the baptism of the Holy Spirit. I promised God that if I found the baptism in Scripture I would believe it. As I began to research the subject throughout the Bible, guess what happened. I prayed for the Lord to forgive me because I had not known the truth. My conscience came alive and I accepted the truth instantly. The Lord then baptized me in His Holy Spirit. I no longer had a seared conscience. At one time I had believed a lie, causing my conscience to become seared. But God's Word took away the searing and caused my conscience to come alive.

VIOLATION OF THE CONSCIENCE

Each person has the ability to know right from wrong and good from evil. This ability is a built-in monitor in the form of the conscienc, which God has created in each of us. In the Bible we are told the conscience bears witness to the Holy Spirit and the Holy Spirit bears witness to our conscience. We are without excuse. When God's Word is before us, our conscience also bears witness to His truths. Our conscience is able to memorize the Word instantly and cause us to remember it when we are in need of a word from the Lord. If we ignore the guidance and advice God has given us through our conscience—His Holy Spirit or His Word—we violate the conscience and come into sin. But if we follow His guidance, not violating our conscience or breaking His Word, we will experience love, joy, peace, and fellowship in a way we have not known before. Our spiritual growth will become stronger and faster because of the continual watering of the Word in our lives. Sin stunts the spiritual growth of a Christian. But if we obey our conscience we will not walk in sin.

Some people say, "Well, I don't do what those people do." This is sin because they are judging and comparing themselves to other people. We should compare ourselves with Jesus and see what needs working on in our lives. Jesus is our example for living, not each other.

In the Bible, Paul says he has walked toward man and God in all good conscience. I believe God wants us all to walk in good conscience. If you are unable to do so, pray to the Lord to help you walk in good conscience. The Lord is faithful to hear and answer our prayers. Walking in good conscience would cause a change in people's attitudes. Temper tantrums would go right out the window. Husbands and wives would not fight anymore.

Some Christians today walk in the sin of violating their consciences and what they do with that violation. Even though they may be in deep trouble with the Lord, He has provided a way for us to learn how to walk above sin. I am not referring to perfection, but how we can walk above sin. Walking in guidance of the conscience causes us to be in obedience to God. Because of our obedience, we will have joy, peace, and love. We will have all that God has for us, including the full flow of His Holy Spirit because the Holy Spirit is given to those who obey.

> *Lord, I pray that I will not harden my heart and that You will teach me to obey my conscience. I ask You, Holy Spirit, to come into my life and guide me as I walk in conscience to the Word of God. In Jesus' name. Amen.*

Chapter 6
ASSOCIATION WITH ACTIONS

THE CONSCIENCE IS a marvelous thing. It is the divine spark that lights every man that is born into the world. The Bible tells us that Jesus lights every man, and His light and truth come to us through our conscience. When we are washed in the blood of Jesus, our conscience becomes keen and perceptive to His will and His Word. It becomes fine-tuned to the things of God.

Co-perception means association with actions. Perception is the act and process of knowing. I thank God for the conscience because the Bible tells me the conscience will witness to the Holy Spirit. I have a double witness, which comes from God. This co-perception means I know that God knows.

Romans 2:14–15 describes the working of the conscience in lost people. Some people reject verses like these because they say people can be a law unto themselves. But their conscience guides them in what is right and wrong or good and evil according to God's moral standards. Man's mind and his actions are monitored by his conscience. They are either accusing or excusing one another. The conscience comes against the carnal mind. When you are walking in the Spirit and in truth, your conscience will speak to your spiritual mind—the mind of the Spirit. Here we have a two-fold agreement—you and your mind, which is now the renewed mind in the Holy Spirit and the conscience, both in agreement with God.

THE EXERCISE OF CHOICE

In Romans 2, the Bible speaks about the ethical Law of Moses, which includes the gospel. It includes the Word of the Lord for God's people. It is not speaking about the ritual Law of Moses.

God has given us a conscience that is identified with our whole personality. The conscience speaks to every part of our life. It speaks to the rational, reasoning, or sensible part by giving sound judgment. It is the act of willing the will. When our will agrees with God's will we are then able to walk with Him. When two agree they can walk together.

The conscience is the exercise of choice. All of us make choices each day of our lives. Everything we do is an act of choice. Our conscience influences what we choose to do by providing us sound judgment. We have a choice to either obey or disobey the guidance of our conscience.

THE ACT OF THE WILL

The act of the will is linked to our conscience. The will knows right from wrong and good from evil because the conscience speaks to our will. What we choose is up to us. We either obey the conscience or not. The conscience knows the will of God and speaks to us when we are searching for answers on a certain matter. People will say, "I just don't know. I have two job offers and I don't know which one to take." But you know; God has chosen one for you. He has ordained it. There is a right one and a wrong one. Through His Holy Spirit and your conscience, He will tell you He has ordained these good works for you to walk in. This means your life is preplanned. It is important that we find the will of God and walk in it.

When people are not hearing what the Lord is saying they end up making wrong choices, and as a result, some fall into self-pity. They have what's called a "pity party" for themselves. I know their conscience must surely have spoken to them about their pity party. The Bible tells us to stand fast; having done all things, stand. (See Ephesians 6:13.) It does not say go feel sorry for yourself. In joy, sorrow, fear, or hate, our mind is not to rule us, not in any of these emotional experiences. Our thoughts will either accuse or excuse us. (See Romans 2:14–15.)

BEING A REPRESENTATIVE

God created the conscience to be used. The conscience comes with absolute authority from God because it is part of creation.

> And God said, Let us make man in our image, after our likeness: and let them have dominion over the fish of the sea, and over the fowl of the air, and over the cattle, and over all the earth, and over every creeping thing that creepeth upon the earth. So God created man in his own image, in the image of God created he him; male and female created he them.
>
> —GENESIS 1:26–27

The word *image* in Hebrew means "phantom, a representative in likeness, and a concrete example."[1] *Concrete* refers to the actual thing or substance. God gave to man His actual substance for revealing right from wrong and good from evil. When Adam and Eve ate the fruit of the tree God had commanded them not to eat, both Adam and Eve instantly

57

knew they had sinned. They had never seen sin before. They had always walked with God, in perfection. They walked with God having a clean conscience. This is the secret to our walk with the Lord—a clean conscience.

Listening to a clean conscience, you hear, "This is the way. Walk ye in it." A clean conscience allows you to rise above sin and begin hearing positive guidance from the Holy Spirit. You mature past the part of, "No, do not do this. This is sin." Because you listen and obey your conscience and the Holy Spirit, you arrive at a new level in the Lord. No longer are you burdened with wrong and evil because you automatically walk in the light of the Lord, knowing and doing what is good and right according to His ways. This is how Adam and Eve walked with the Lord before the Fall. They walked in perfection with God because He had created them this way. When sin came into the world through disobedience to God, it brought the burden of knowing wrong and evil.

The plus-side of our conscience is a tremendous thing that many people do not experience. They have not realized this is what God has made available to them since the time of Creation. God has made our conscience to be our supreme practical guide in all things. If we choose to disobey this guidance, the Holy Spirit will not guide us.

When we are in disobedience to our conscience, it then leads us back to God in an effort to restore our walk with Him. The conscience will say, "Do you know what you need to do? You need to back up, turn around, repent, and get right with God." Obeying the conscience brings us into right relationship with God.

Obedience to the conscience does not take the place of the Holy Spirit. If we refuse to obey the simple things the conscience talks to us about, we will never have a chance to obey the Holy Spirit. The Holy Spirit is not going to guide us past something the conscience has already talked to us about. Our conscience, plus the Holy Spirit, is a sure path to spiritual growth. We cannot help but grow up in Christ.

LIVE THE HIGH LIFE

Not only did Paul write about the conscience more than anyone else, he also used his conscience to guide him in all his ministry: "And Paul, earnestly beholding the council, said, Men and brethren, I have lived in all good conscience before God until this day" (Acts 23:1). Can you imagine such a statement? When you can say what Paul has said in this verse, your life can live on a high plain that brings you higher and higher unto the Lord, because He has a sure Word. He wrote a sure Word. If anyone had a reason to rebel, it was Paul. He was thrown into prison for nothing, beaten, and shipwrecked. All of these things came upon him, and he could have said, "I thought I was walking with You. What's wrong, God? Don't You understand that all of this is happening to me?"

Have you ever found yourself talking to the Lord this way? Maybe you begin to reason a little and then your conscience tells you, "Shut your mouth. Get right with God." To be able to hear and submit to your conscience causes the Holy Spirit to flood you with the presence of the Lord. The conscience must always be obeyed.

OBEDIENCE BRINGS REVELATION

The fundamental principle for Christian ethics is that we must always obey our conscience. Only after obeying our conscience does revelation come. God will not reveal further steps in our life until our conscience is clear. We have seen

59

in earlier chapters great men of God who followed their consciences and subsequently were blessed with much revelation from the Lord. At the Council of Worms, Martin Luther was on trial for not going against his conscience. Many have said the Reformation was a revival of the conscience, brought about by Luther's convictions of his own conscience in the light of God's Word. In those days the revival of the church spread across the world as a result of Luther's stand. When the officials of the Catholic Church told Luther to stop making waves and ordered him to recant his teaching and sermons, Luther stood before them and said his conscience was bound to God's Word. He told them he could not, nor did he wish to recall his sermons or writings. Because of Luther's conscience and the stand he took, revival swept the land. Luther was willing to die for what was right. He stood there knowing the death penalty. Luther was later saved by a German prince.

Many have described the Reformation as an awakening of the conscience. Whether we are children by birth or by creation, our conscience speaks to us and lets us know what God expects. He does not leave us wandering around in confusion.

> Now the Spirit speaketh expressly, that in the latter times some shall depart from the faith, giving heed to seducing spirits, and doctrines of devils; Speaking lies in hypocrisy; having their conscience seared with a hot iron.
> —1 TIMOTHY 4:1–2

Our conscience becomes seared when we hear someone who teaches lies as though they were truths from the Bible. The Greek translation for the verse above says the conscience is put out of action. I had this happen to me. I had been taught there was no such thing as the baptism of the Holy Spirit. My conscience was seared in that part of my life. People would talk to me about the Holy Spirit and speaking in tongues but I would not receive it.

Our conscience can be alive in every point except for the one where it is seared with unbelief. Speaking lies and hypocrisy means speaking a lie as if it is truth. But praise the Lord, His Word wakes up and revives a seared conscience. We see in the previous verse there were those who had departed from the faith. They were speaking on the doctrine of demons. This is why we should be careful who we hear preaching and teaching. There are some preachers on television you should not watch at all. They are putting seeds in your mind. They are the kind of seeds that can sear a conscience with false doctrine. If you listen to these preachers long enough, before long you will be speaking the words you heard them say. You are better off listening to the Word of God.

Father God, I want a revival of my conscience, that I may be a Christian who walks in the Spirit and in truth. I pray that my conscience might be bound in the Word of God. In Jesus' name. Amen.

61

Chapter 7
REVIEWING THE CONSCIENCE

MORE AND MORE as I study the conscience, I believe one of the most basic principles for a Christian to understand is the operation of his or her conscience. When we know the operation of our conscience we are tremendously ahead in the wisdom and knowledge of the Lord. When God's Word is written in our hearts and engraved upon our minds, the conscience is renewed and washed by the blood of Jesus Christ and the water of the Word. No longer is there a reason for us to say, "I wish I knew if this were God or not. I wish I knew if this were right or wrong." When we learn to listen to our conscience we know the right direction to walk.

The Bible teaches us that God made us in His image and in His likeness. He wants us to walk in knowledge. Our lives are ones of co-perception. We travel through life with God working with us. His voice and the voice of our conscience help to direct, guide, start, and stop the things we do, say, or think. What a tremendous thing it is for people who have a sharp conscience to always be walking by their consciences. They can literally tell right from wrong every time. The reason most Christians cannot is because they have stopped their consciences. They have run over their conscience so many times that they do not trust themselves. They say no so many times they can hardly hear the conscience.

63

Our conscience is not meant to take the place of the Holy Spirit. Obeying the conscience brings us to the Holy Spirit. It takes us to holiness and righteousness. Listening and obeying the conscience always takes us to the Lord God. Through co-perception we recognize God's hand in guiding us through life. We are able to see completely, understand, be aware, and informed of right and wrong.

DIRECT GUIDANCE FROM GOD

When we take the first step of obeying the conscience, the next step is direct guidance from the Lord. Those who continually ignore their conscience and the Word of God do not get to the second step. Obedience to the first step always brings us to flowing in the Holy Spirit. The conscience of a born-again Christian accepts only the Word of God as truth. When we are faced with a decision of right and wrong or good and evil, the conscience agrees with the leading of the Holy Spirit. Our conscience becomes a witness to the Holy Spirit and the Word that is in our hearts. Sometimes we do not yet understand the Word that is in our hearts. Meditating on God's Word will help our understanding.

But who meditates anymore? In Hebrew, *meditate* actually means "to mumble." Sometimes a certain verse will stay in our mind and on our heart and we find ourselves repeating it over and over. This is mumbling or meditating. Our conscience teaches us how to meditate on God's Word.

> This book of the law shall not depart out of thy mouth; but thou shalt meditate therein day and night, that thou mayest observe to do according to all that is written therein: for then thou shalt make thy way prosperous, and then thou shalt have good success.
>
> —JOSHUA 1:8

64

Some are not listening to the Word or to their conscience. If they would take the first step, their consciences would teach them that the Word is life. The conscience never supersedes the Word. It becomes a slave to God's Word. Hearing the truth in our conscience and knowing that God knows we know this truth is what is meant by co-perception. We are provided a sure witness of truth by God through the conscience and the Holy Spirit witnessing to each other on what is right and wrong or good and evil. If we refuse their witness, we come into rebellion and direct disobedience to the Lord.

> For when the Gentiles, which have not the law, do by nature the things contained in the law, these, having not the law, are a law unto themselves.
> —ROMANS 2:14

The phrase *They do by nature* in verse 14 means they obey the conscience. Have you ever received a witness from within? This is your conscience speaking to you. Once you obey your conscience, you begin to learn the voice of the Holy Spirit, which is your second witness. Disobeying the first witness causes you not to hear the second witness. You drown His voice out with rebellion.

> Which shew the work of the law written in their hearts, their conscience also bearing witness, and their thoughts the mean while accusing or else excusing one another.
> —ROMANS 2:15

Verse 15 tells us the witness of the conscience also affects our thought life. We are able to recognize right or wrong thoughts with the help of our conscience.

HAVE THE MIND OF CHRIST

The Christian's mind is like a container. It holds the mind of Christ. The Bible tells us we must be renewed in the spirit of our mind. What this means is that when we hear the will of God or righteousness and holiness or God speaking, the conscience says, "Amen." The conscience witnesses to our mind. The conscience agrees with the Word and the will of God because we have the Word inside us. Isn't this a tremendous thing we carry around in us? The will of God.

Do you know what it is to have what is called "a check" in your spirit? It is when the conscience says no and the Holy Spirit says no, but you go ahead anyway and do that certain thing. What happens at this point is you fall out of fellowship. Right then your fellowship with God stops because you disobey your conscience and the Holy Spirit. The Word He gave you was disobeyed.

GROWING UP IN CHRIST

We must always follow our conscience. It will bring us into an ethical walk—God's walk. The conscience does not take the place of the Holy Spirit, but rather it leads us to the Holy Spirit and living the Word. Following the conscience is a sure path to spiritual growth. Each of us can be spiritual giants if we would only begin to slow down and take time to hear what our conscience is saying. Many times we are in too much of a hurry and we do not take time to listen to what our conscience is saying. Often we end up in a mess. But here again the conscience leads us out of the mess and to the Holy Spirit.

We all want to be used mightily by God. The proof we have of those who obeyed their conscience in all areas and became mighty men of God are the apostle Paul and Martin Luther. These men were spiritual giants because they took the first step in obeying their consciences.

Guarding your conscience is as important as listening to it. Guard it against untruths spoken as though they were truth. If we begin to believe a lie that is spoken as though it were a truth of God, our conscience becomes seared and dead to that particular area spoken about. We are then unable to hear guidance from our conscience because we believe the lie rather than the truth.

> Now the Spirit speaketh expressly, that in the latter times some shall depart from the faith, giving heed to seducing spirits, and doctrines of devils.
>
> —1 Timothy 4:1

In the verse above the Bible is not speaking about the Last Days when it says "in the latter times." It is speaking about from here on out. Some will depart from faith because they have listened to devils talking and teaching about other devils. Jesus taught us that devils come in tribes. There are tribes of devils that bring lust and sickness and teach religious things. When the disciples were unable to cast the epileptic spirit out of a boy, Jesus said, "This kind can come forth by nothing, but by prayer and fasting" (Mark 9:29). The word *kind* in this verse means "tribe." Jesus was saying, "This tribe is hard to dislodge." Demons will get ahold of a person and teach them contrary to Scripture. The people these demons inhabit speak lies and hypocrisy because they have listened to religious things taught by these demons. The people speaking lies and hypocrisy know they are doing wrong. Their consciences have become seared.

> Jesus answered and said unto them, Ye do err, not knowing the scriptures, nor the power of God.
>
> —MATTHEW 22:29

It is important for us to learn Scripture and let Scripture teach our conscience. The more we are renewed in the spirit of our mind through the Word, the more we are able to walk in spontaneous divine guidance. God did not intend for us to stop and pray about everything we do. He intends for His will to flow through us. When you were lost, did you have to be taught how to live a lost life? No.

> For when ye were the servants of sin, ye were free from righteousness. What fruit had ye then in those things whereof ye are now ashamed? for the end of those things is death.
>
> —ROMANS 6:20–21

In the verse above we see the people were free from righteousness. They lived a life of unrighteousness spontaneously.

> But now being made free from sin, and become servants to God, ye have your fruit unto holiness, and the end everlasting life.
>
> —ROMANS 6:22

Fruit is the growth of a healthy tree. Spiritual fruit is the growth produced from a healthy Christian. The spiritual fruit cannot help but spring forth. You have never heard a pear tree say, "I sure have to give pears this year. Oh, God, can I have pears this year?" If everything is right with the pear tree, fruit automatically comes forth. This is the type of thing we Christians go through. If everything is right, we are going to have spiritual fruit. We can still pray for fruit, but it is better when we walk void of offense in our conscience before God and man. This way we cannot help but bear fruit. Our conscience will always bear witness and will always bring us to God. God will then bring us into the fullness of His life.

It would be quite an experiment to see a group of people living by their conscience and the Word written on their hearts. People living this way could see firsthand how much the Holy Spirit would bring them into. Thank God for the Bible. You know, the Bible does not do us any good under our arm. We have to eat His Word. We must digest it and have it become a part of us. Similar to the process of eating food, when we eat the Word and then meditate on it, it becomes part of us as we digest it. Then we are renewed in the spirit of our mind.

Father, how I thank You for my conscience. I ask You to teach me to listen and obey my conscience. In Jesus' name. Amen.

69

Chapter 8

FOLLOWING OUR CONSCIENCE

To FOLLOW OUR conscience is always to follow and not resist. This sounds like the same thing, but it is not. We are able to follow our conscience and resist it at the same time, but what we end up doing is putting a damper on the flow of the Word of the Lord in our life.

Some people say, "Well, I always obey the Lord after the battle. First I have my fling and then later I follow God." This is not following the conscience. This is simply resisting it. Following our conscience completely allows the door to open for further revelation from God.

> Therefore to him that knoweth to do good, and doeth it not, to him it is sin.
>
> —JAMES 4:17

The Greek translation for the word *sin* is "to miss the mark." Refusing to do what we know is right causes us to miss His life. It is impossible for us to receive further revelation when we refuse to walk in the revelation at hand. Obedience to the conscience opens revelation from the Lord. Some people say, "I have no revelation." First they must see if they are fighting their conscience. All of us know what is right and wrong. We need to obey the conscience. Why would God want to give us revelation when we are not walking in the revelation we have already?

Have you heard how some preach the gospel today? They say, "You ought to help poor old Jesus out. You ought to go ahead and get saved and help Him out." The gospel should not be preached this way at all. When the gospel is preached with the convicting power of the Holy Spirit, we find out that we are the ones being helped. We find out that we have a cleansed conscience, we have the living Word, and a living Savior. Praise God! Except by the grace of God, we can point to any man that is wallowing in sin and see a picture of where we would be without Jesus. The enemy can take those who are not saved at will. The whole world lies in wickedness.

I have heard some people say there are nice sinners and poor sinners. There is no such thing. They all are in wickedness. The devil has his way with them.

We must remember that before the Lord gives us revelation, we first must obey our conscience. We should be able to say what Martin Luther said. "My conscience is bound to the Word of God."[1] If Luther had ignored his conscience, his ministry would have come to a stop. Even though the charges against him would have been dropped and he would have been welcomed back into the Catholic Church, he would have given up the fellowship of the Holy Spirit. He would have given up the peace of God. He would also have given up tribulation, because the Bible says, "For verily, when we were with you, we told you before that we should suffer tribulation; even as it came to pass" (1 Thess. 3:4).

RECOGNIZING YOUR CONSCIENCE AS SERVANT

With all this about the conscience, what is really being said? Basically we are not alone. We are servants to whomsoever we yield to obey. The Holy Spirit and our conscience guide us in our yielding. We do not have to flip a coin every time. Our conscience shows us which direction to yield in.

Recently I was in a situation when my conscience said, "Do not yield yourself to this." I saw other Christians yielding themselves to it. But my conscience would not allow it so I obeyed my conscience. When we walk with our conscience we can walk through fire and not even have the smell of smoke on us. Our conscience will keep us out of trouble. Our conscience is our servant because Christ is the Lord of our conscience. Every time the Lord speaks, the conscience says, "Amen. I agree with that."

Once I had a Christian brother visiting our church that said he saw us walking in knowledge. All any of us have to do is listen to our conscience a little and we can walk in lots of knowledge and revelation gifts. The grace of God is with us and the Word is with us. The Lord Jesus Christ is the Master of the conscience. We must always obey Jesus. The conscience will always obey the Lord. When we obey we have a double witness.

Our union with Jesus involves a progressive walk. We grow up into His image and likeness. As we grow we receive training from the conscience through the Word. The conscience is filled with God's moral laws, but it continues to need training in spiritual things. We must be trained.

Some people say, "All we need to walk with the Lord is faith." We need more than faith if we want to walk with Him.

> Holding faith, and a good conscience; which some having put away concerning faith have made shipwreck.
> —1 Timothy 1:19

73

It takes a pure faith and a pure conscience to walk with the Lord.

YOUR CONSCIENCE AND THE BIBLE

Some people have said, "I don't need the Bible. I'll just listen to my conscience." We do need the Bible. We need to feed upon the Word of God. The conscience will never take the place of the Bible because God uses His Word to train the conscience.

Our conscience always agrees with the Bible. It is not meant to take the place of God's Word. "So then faith cometh by hearing, and hearing by the word of God" (Rom. 10:17). The Word works. If we were to preach to the lost about hell, fire, and damnation, they would get faith to help them out of damnation. Be faithful with the Word, not ideas.

> For it is better, if the will of God be so, that ye suffer for well doing, than for evil doing. For Christ also hath once suffered for sins, the just for the unjust, that he might bring us to God, being put to death in the flesh, but quickened by the Spirit: By which also he went and preached unto the spirits in prison.
>
> —1 PETER 3:17–19

After His death Jesus did not go down into hell and preach salvation to the disobedient who were there. He went down and proclaimed their doom.

> Which sometime were disobedient, when once the longsuffering of God waited in the days of Noah, while the ark was a preparing, wherein few, that is, eight souls were saved by water. The like figure whereunto even baptism doth also now save us (not the putting

away of the filth of the flesh, but the answer of a good conscience toward God,) by the resurrection of Jesus Christ.

—1 PETER 3:20–21

Your conscience will agree with God, and it will not leave you alone until you are washed in the blood of Jesus Christ. The conscience never turns off. It will wake you up and talk to you in the middle of the night. Some people are looking for peace, and peace only comes when the conscience is washed in the blood of Jesus.

In the previous verses the same water that killed the people saved Noah and his family. Jesus Christ is our Ark. When Noah was building the ark the Lord told him to "pitch within and without." The Hebrew translation says "within and without with atonement." In every way the ark was a picture of Jesus.

When I was in prayer to the Lord I asked Him to help me have an ethical walk. The answer I received by revelation of Jesus Christ was that I must have the Word of God within me. I must retrain my conscience in the Word. You can, too.

Paul, an apostle of Jesus Christ by the commandment of God our Saviour, and Lord Jesus Christ, which is our hope; Unto Timothy, my own son in the faith: Grace, mercy, and peace, from God our Father and Jesus Christ our Lord. As I besought thee to abide still at Ephesus, when I went into Macedonia, that thou mightest charge some that they teach no other doctrine, Neither give heed to fables and endless genealogies, which minister questions, rather than godly edifying which is in faith: so do. Now the end of the commandment is charity out

75

of a pure heart, and of a good conscience, and of faith unfeigned: From which some having swerved have turned aside unto vain jangling.

—1 TIMOTHY 1:1–6

NO RESPECTER OF PERSONS

Our conscience is so tied to the Word of God that it alone will bring us to the fullness of Jesus Christ as we go through the Word. This is why an honest preacher, regardless of his denomination and if he is honest with himself and God, will come into the fullness of God. Many people preach way past their experience. They see a truth and preach it. They gain that truth.

Some people are unable to preach certain things because their denomination will not allow it. Their conscience tells them yes in preaching the message, but they disobey the conscience and obey their denomination. Christians who obey go on with the Lord. Those who hold us back from God should be left alone so that we can have a pure heart, good conscience, and faith. Men will snare us if we let them. It is important that we do not hold men and their traditions in respect instead of God and His Word.

When Paul went to Jerusalem he made the statement, "There was James and there was Peter." He said both men were highly thought of, but God respects no man's person. In other words Paul did not dare hold James and Peter in esteem above anyone else in the church because they all have the same Savior, the same Jesus Christ. I believe the only way we might hold someone in esteem is if the person is faithful in comparison to another person who is unfaithful.

Obeying the Word and our conscience causes our faith to

release in a powerful way. When we do not obey, the release of faith turns into "vain janglings."

Training our conscience in the Word of God causes us to mature. Being in a New Testament church that preaches God's Word also helps us to mature. A New Testament church is one in which all the gifts are available and there are apostles, prophets, pastors, teachers, elders, deacons, helps, and governments. There should be all nine of the gifts ministering in your church. It is still possible for a Christian to grow in a church without these, but they will not be brought into maturity. A Christian can grow and train his conscience through his study of the Word.

HOW TO PRAY ABOUT YOUR CONSCIENCE

"Pray for us: for we trust we have a good conscience, in all things willing to live honestly" (Heb. 13:18). Some say, "Please pray for me." But I know at the time they ask for prayer that they are not obeying their conscience. It is tragic that as important as the conscience is, it is not taught much. The conscience should be shown its rightful place: putting people in conflict so that the Holy Spirit can use the conscience to put people under conviction of sin in their lost condition. The Catholic Catechism teaches on the conscience, but it is the last thing taught.

> Likewise must the deacons be grave, not doubletongued,
> not given to much wine, not greedy of filthy lucre;
> Holding the mystery of the faith in a pure conscience.
> —1 TIMOTHY 3:8–9

There are those who have the mystery of faith but do not have a clear conscience. What a tremendous position the conscience will play. When we do not have a clear conscience we are not qualified to be a deacon. Stop and think about that. How can a person consistently fight for God with a clear conscience, but have strife in his or her life? It cannot be done. We can have the Word and our faith, but to keep that life we must have the conscience in control.

> I thank God, whom I serve from my forefathers with pure conscience, that without ceasing I have remembrance of thee in my prayers night and day.
> —2 TIMOTHY 1:3

The one thing in this verse that proves Paul's point is his saying he serves God with a pure conscience. Now he might have said he serves God with real faith, and that does say something. But it does not say as much nor have the impact as having served with a pure conscience.

PAUL THE APOSTLE'S RULE OF LIFE

Paul was a successful minister whose apostolic ministry was a success. His success was not due to his education or that he was not married. What made Paul a success was what he was able to say time and time again—that he never violated his conscience toward God or man. This was his rule of life. He was sold out to Jesus. If we never violate our conscience, we are already sold out to Jesus.

God does not look at success in the way that man does. Success in God's estimation is someone who is faithful, someone He can count on. Living right before the Lord all the time comes from listening to the teaching of our conscience. Doing this brings peace and righteousness. Taking that first step in obeying our conscience brings us rest and more revelation from God.

> And they neither found me in the temple disputing with any man, neither raising up the people, neither in the synagogues, nor in the city: Neither can they prove the things whereof they now accuse me. But this I confess unto thee, that after the way which they call heresy, so worship I the God of my fathers, believing all things which are written in the law and in the prophets: And have hope toward God, which they themselves also allow, that there shall be a resurrection of the dead, both of the just and unjust. And herein do I exercise myself, to have always a conscience void of offence toward God, and toward men.
>
> —ACTS 24:12–16

In the previous verses Paul is saying that if you want to know his creed, it was that he trained his conscience in the Old Testament. Verse 14 tells where he trained his conscience. He says because he believes what is written in the Law and the Prophets, his conscience will guide him. He continues saying his conscience is void of offense toward God and men. Never has his conscience spoken to him that he was wrong. Some preach that Paul never sinned once he was born again. It is hard to sin when a person always obeys his or her conscience. The conscience always speaks to us if we get into sin. It speaks before, during, and afterward.

LIVING A LIFE WITHOUT SIN

It does not take a great man or a little man to live without sin. It takes a person who lives in obedience to his or her conscience. "And herein do I exercise myself, to have always a conscience void of offence toward God, and toward men" (Acts 24:16).

There was a time when Paul disobeyed his conscience. He

79

went against what his conscience told him, but he always made it right. When our conscience troubles us, the only way to get it right is to be washed in the blood of the Lamb. We will never have peace until we do this. Once we begin to hear our conscience, the Holy Spirit and the voice of our conscience become one word. First you will hear the conscience and then you will hear the Holy Spirit. After you are used to obeying your conscience, they blend together, and you have the same witness all the time. This is scriptural.

Some people say, "I don't hear the voice of the Lord." What they are really saying is they never listen to their conscience. The Bible says that the two become one—the conscience witnessing in the Holy Spirit. If the conscience is witnessing in the Holy Spirit you only hear one word. You hear your conscience and the Holy Spirit at the same time. Each time the Holy Spirit speaks, the conscience says, "Amen. That's right."

We know that our conscience is not meant to take the place of the Holy Spirit or the written Word of God. We must be bound to the written covenant, which is God's Holy Word, in all ways. Our duty as a Christian is to read it. God left His Word for us to study, read, know, and obey. If you are unsure about any of this, just ask your conscience.

Father, I thank You that You have given me a conscience. You have given me Your Word and Your life. May I walk in it always. In Jesus' name. Amen.

Chapter 9

KNOWING MORAL VALUE

THE GREEK TRANSLATION of the New Testament helps us to understand the conscience and its work in a Christian.[1] It says the conscience is to arouse us as if from death. It is to revive, restore to new life, and give new life by co-perception. The conscience is to work alongside us. This is what is meant by co-perception. The conscience works alongside us in knowing moral value. We are brought to life and shown moral values at the same time. The conscience shows us right from wrong and good from evil. It is immediate recognition. Co-perception causes us to see completely, understand, to become aware, and informed. We are able to recognize the conscience and its leading. All of these things happen because we are made in the image and likeness of God. Because God is holy and righteous, He has placed the ability in us to recognize holiness and righteousness. This ability is through our conscience and co-perception.

In previous chapters we have seen that the unsaved have a conscience. (See Romans 2:14–15.) Those of us who are Christians have had our conscience washed with the blood of Jesus. When God created mankind He created them knowing His will through their consciences. When we look into the covenant that is given to the New Testament church, we find that God writes His laws in our hearts and engraves

81

them upon our minds. This is done through the work of the conscience. These are ethical laws and not ritual laws.

The conscience is given to us to govern us and keep us walking with the Lord. When we confess our sins to the Lord He is faithful to cleanse us in His blood. This includes the cleansing of our conscience. Once the conscience is cleansed it ceases to trouble us of the sin we committed. We have peace with ourselves and peace with God.

UNDERSTANDING CONSCIENCE

Today we have what is called a charismatic revival. But you know, we cannot have a revival until people have a revival in the conscience. This will help them to be obedient to the Word of God. Most of what is called revival is really the flesh. There is so much sin mixed in with it. God will not bless His people when they walk in sin. Some people take the Word of God and pick and choose passages to obey in a way it was not intended.

When a person's conscience is seared it will not speak to him or her on certain subjects. It does not speak in the area it is seared. Listening to others speaking lies in hypocrisy sears the conscience. The Bible tells us in the Last Days there will be those who speak lies in hypocrisy. Some will believe what they hear and will be seduced by devils and taught doctrines of demons. But our conscience bears witness only to the Word of God—when we listen to it. Our conscience always brings us to God. The conscience does not take the place of the Word or God's Holy Spirit. Instead it brings us to the doorstep of the Word. It delivers us to the feet of Jesus.

Our conscience only has to hear the Word once to be trained. It is able to bear witness immediately. The Word is the training ground for the conscience. Through training we then know how to approach the Lord. We know how to walk with Him and learn His ways.

We all have a choice of walking with the Lord or searing our conscience. We can either walk with the Lord or walk under condemnation. God has given us everything we need to walk with Him.

Lord, I ask that I would have revival in my conscience and walk according to the Word and will of God obeying the conscience. In Jesus' name. Amen.

Chapter 10
OBEYING THE CHECKS
AND BALANCES

*And Paul, earnestly beholding the council,
said, men and brethren, I have lived in all
good conscience before God until this day.*
—ACTS 23:1

THE PEOPLE PAUL is talking to in the verse above did not know a thing about his new doctrine. All they knew was that he preached Jesus. Those he spoke to were the rulers and people in the temples. Paul explained to them that in this new faith a person was able to live a much closer life to the Lord than in the old covenant. The statement Paul made about living in all good conscience toward God and man was what caused the people in the temple to listen. They understood what he meant because they knew they were not living in good conscience.

> And herein do I exercise myself, to have always a conscience void of offence toward God and toward men.
> —ACTS 24:16

I believe we need a revival of the conscience. There was a time when no one wanted to admit they had the baptism of the Holy Spirit. In fact, if someone were to mention they had received the baptism they were kicked out of their church.

85

This happened to me. I was the pastor of a church when I received the baptism of the Holy Spirit. Either because the people were not interested or they just did not believe the Word of God, they turned against me for having received the baptism of the Holy Spirit.

DIVINE AUTHORITY

If we had a revival of the conscience today, people would be void of offense toward God and men. It would bring them into unity as a whole. Something we must remember is that the conscience never takes the place of the Holy Spirit. It is meant to bring us to the Word and the Holy Spirit.

When we make wrong choices and enter into evil, either by choosing no when we should have chosen yes or yes when we should have chosen no, our conscience is there to arrest or stop us. The conscience will arouse us out of the passivity of sin that brings us into the wrong place. At the seat of the conscience is God's divine authority. We were created by God and given a conscience that ministers His truth and ways so that we may be void of offense toward God and man. The key is for us to stop, listen, and heed what the conscience is saying. It will always witness to the truth and ways of God in His Word.

SEARCH THE WORD

In Romans 9:1 Paul goes a step further in obeying his conscience. His first step was being void of offense. This step puts a person on neutral ground. In other words, Paul is able to be void of offense by always obeying his conscience and being good to people. This point is a launching platform or neutral place because it sets you in a place ready to take the next step.

Romans 9:1 speaks of a tremendous walk: "I say the truth in Christ, I lie not, my conscience also bearing me witness in the Holy Ghost." This verse tells us Paul had a witness from his conscience. His conscience bears witness in the Holy Spirit. When our conscience speaks to us and we obey, it then bears witness when the Holy Spirit speaks.

> For our rejoicing is this, the testimony of our conscience, that in simplicity and godly sincerity, not with fleshly wisdom, but by the grace of God, we have had our conversation in the world, and more abundantly to you-ward.
>
> —2 CORINTHIANS 1:12

What a tremendous revelation this is when we find we have the testimony of the conscience. What was Paul saying in the verse above? He proved he never became bogged down in religion. He stayed in simplicity, godly sincerity, and not with fleshly wisdom. If fleshly wisdom were taken out of the preaching and teaching done today and the simplicity and godly sincerity put back in, we would have revival on top of revival! If each minister in the New Testament churches or Christian arena were to abide by this verse for one year, we would see a great transformation in them, the people, and the church. Christians would know right is right and wrong is wrong. I know it is the Holy Spirit that wells up inside me when I hear preachers say, "Well, after all, we are in the twenty-first century and what they had in the first century is not sufficient for today because we have different problems." The problem is still sin! It is still rebellion! The problem is still one of doing your own thing and not walking with God. There is nothing new under the sun. Rebellion is still rebellion; flesh is still flesh; hate is still hate; and sin is still sin.

THE TESTIMONY OF OUR CONSCIENCE

As you move into your own ministry you will reach more people when you are sincere and keep the message simple. The Bible tells us that Jesus asked what the people had come out to hear. The people were expecting some great revelation, but what Jesus preached was righteousness. He preached against sin. He preached about being obedient to the Word and to the Father. He did not have any great revelation to give to them, rather He told them where they stood and what they could do to come forth.

John the Baptist preached one of the greatest sermons ever recorded in the Bible. It is one sentence of about four or five words. He preached that sermon and got his head cut off. But John's conscience was clear. He did not compromise. Each word he spoke in that sermon rang in his ears and spoke in his heart. It was the testimony of his conscience.

> But have renounced the hidden things of dishonesty, not walking in craftiness, nor handling the word of God deceitfully; but by manifestation of the truth commending ourselves to every man's conscience in the sight of God.
>
> —2 CORINTHIANS 4:2

In the above verse Paul states the manner in which he lives before God and preaches the Word. In the statement "commending ourselves to every man's conscience," Paul is saying it is possible for man's conscience to know the character and ways of other men. When we learn to listen to our conscience, we can then find out if a minister is walking in all good conscience. Our conscience lets us know if he really believes what he preaches. Do you realize that when you are dealing with someone and you suspect deceit or craftiness that it is your conscience that tells you these things?

A few years ago we ministered to a woman who had a house for runaway teenagers. She was trying to bring these kids to the Lord. We warned her to keep a particular boy and girl apart. She acknowledged our warning and said she was alerted to the problem already and was keeping them apart. Her conscience had told her what was going on between the kids. It is the same as your conscience telling you when someone is pure.

Our conscience does so much for us. It is important we always listen to it by renouncing the hidden things of dishonesty, not walking in craftiness and not handling the Word of God deceitfully.

When my ministry team and I go out to minister, many times people come to just check us out. These people do not have the gifts in operation. After we are there a short while, the Holy Spirit begins to bear witness to their consciences that what we are ministering is the uncompromised Word of God. One time someone came up to me and asked, "What's your angle?" I replied, "What do you mean?" He then said, "Well, the meetings are over and you never made a drive for money. So, what are you after? People always have a motive. What's your motive?" I answered, "I am obeying the Lord. Is there anything wrong with that? God sent me." Then I turned it around and asked him if he was receiving and obeying the Lord.

> Knowing therefore the terror of the Lord, we persuade men; but we are made manifest unto God; and I trust also are made manifest in your conscience.
> —2 Corinthians 5:11

Paul wrote the previous verse to Corinth telling them that he was transparent and not hiding anything; he was not ministering with a secret motive. He told them he knew the fear of the Lord. He knew God's judgment is for the righteous as well as the unrighteous. Paul says even though he persuades men he is visible to God, he manifests to God; his conscience bears him witness and trusts that the conscience of the people in Corinth will do the same thing in checking Paul to see that he is what he says he is.

OUTWARDLY AND INWARDLY CLEAN

We have an elementary teaching on home life for the people in our church. It is a simple teaching about a person keeping himself clean. We teach the importance of presenting oneself outwardly clean and then inwardly clean, things like combing the hair and having pride in the way a person presents him or herself. What shows on the outside begins in the heart. Some do not care about their outward appearance. They have no pride in how they look. When I say *pride* I am not talking about a sinful pride or pridefulness. It is a pride that if someone saw you dirty, filthy, and unclean, you would be morally ashamed.

There is a pride that is within us to present ourselves right. When this becomes a way of life we are able to walk in a clear conscience inwardly and outwardly, in our ministry and in our everyday life. We are able to enter into a real rest, having peace with God. We have a rest in that we do not have to defend ourselves. All we have to do is preach the Word of the Lord, and try as they might, others will check us out and find their conscience shows them nothing. These people do not know that it is their conscience that is checking us out. Their conscience says, "This is all right. You can trust them."

What does the conscience tell us? Not only must we have a clear conscience ourselves, but we also must pass the test of someone else's conscience. An example would be if you are listening to a minister and all of a sudden he gets a little edgy and goes off on the broken part of a program. You are not able to prove a thing he is preaching in the Word of God. In fact, he is preaching contrary to the Word and your spirit wants to go to pieces. You react this way not because you are smarter than he is, but because your God-given conscience says he is wrong. How many times have you walked away from an automobile salesman or a product on the shelf because all of sudden something told you to back away from it and leave it alone? Obey the checks and balances within you—they are God given. We've seen how Paul demanded his conscience to bear witnesses to his total life. So should we.

BUNYAN'S *HOLY WAR*

John Bunyan was an English preacher in the late 1600s who wrote several books, including one called *Holy War*. This book is a religious allegory with characters that symbolize certain qualities of people and places. Bunyan's book is about Prince Emmanuel, the hero of the story, rescuing and restoring Mr. Recorder in City of Man's Soul. Prince Emmanuel represents Jesus; Mr. Recorder represents the conscience in a lost man; and City of Man's Soul represents man. In the story, Prince Emmanuel enters City of Man's Soul and captures the man's soul. Prince Emmanuel then restores Mr. Recorder to his complete power of attorney, or complete authority. Before Mr. Recorder was restored, City of Man's Soul had mistreated Mr. Recorder and had tried to put him in jail. The following paragraph is an excerpt from Bunyan's *Holy War*. I have also included my comments within brackets.

> Then did the prince call unto the old gentleman [Bunyan is talking about the conscience in a newly saved person] who had afore been the recorded of man's soul, Mr. Conscience by name, and told him for as much as he was well-skilled in the law, and in the government of the town of man's soul. And then thou must Mr. Conscience, you must do this, said the Priest. Confine your teaching to the moral values of the civil and natural things which the Lord's Secretary knoweth [the Lord's Secretary represents the Holy Spirit]. He said, "Now confine thyself to the teaching of morals, virtues, civil and natural things which the Lord's Secretary knoweth; and thou shalt teach this people thou must be his caller and learner even as the rest of man's soul."[1]

The revelation God gave Bunyan about man's conscience is presented in this story. Bunyan is saying that Mr. Conscience has total charge of man's soul. Mr. Conscience knows the laws, governments, and what the Holy Spirit wants from man. When the Holy Spirit speaks, Mr. Conscience and man's soul are both to learn His ways. Bunyan had the revelation of the conscience knowing only the moral law and of the Holy Spirit wanting to teach man all things pertaining to Jesus Christ. Our conscience needs to be trained unto all things.

You Can Walk and Sin Not

How many times have you heard someone say the following? "I can remember a time a few years ago when I had a tremendous experience with the Lord. It lasted two or three days, and I felt like I was on cloud nine. I wish I could remember how to get back to that position." How do you think they got in that position in the first place? It was not by accident.

God did not reach out and push their spiritual button. What happened was they had first been led by their conscience and then by the Holy Spirit into the presence of the Lord. What we need to realize is that the conscience remembers how to get into the presence of the Lord. If these people knew this, their conscience could take them right back again.

There are some people who try to pray themselves through to getting into the Holy Spirit. But by the exercise of our conscience we are led directly into the Spirit, and we stay there most of the time. Those who are praying in order to get into the Holy Spirit are actually battling with themselves. Their desire is to worship and meet with the Lord, but the battle in their heart makes it difficult. They walk in the Spirit for a while and then they walk in the flesh for a while. It does not have to be this way at all! We can stay in the Spirit continually when we follow the leading of our conscience. The conscience guides us to the Word and to the Holy Spirit. We have the testimony of our conscience that we are walking in the Spirit. There are times when you are in the Spirit and a great joy comes over you. You are embraced by the joy of the Lord, but in this great exuberance of joy the flesh begins to creep in. The conscience and the Holy Spirit will keep you in check. Both will tell you, "All right, back away from this." It is all right for us to have joy, as well as anger, without sinning. We can have joy and sin not. We can have every emotion without sin.

> Now the end of the commandment is charity out of a pure heart, and of a good conscience, and faith unfeigned: From which some having swerved have turned aside unto vain jangling.
> —1 Timothy 1:5–6

93

We see from the previous verse that when we swerve from a good conscience, we immediately end up in "vain jangling." When the conscience is not right, we will not have the testimony of a good conscience. "Vain jangling" in that verse is akin to what is called playing church. It is empty talk with no purpose. Being in this condition causes a person to be under conviction of sin and not presentable to the Lord.

The Lord revealed much to Paul about the conscience. Having a good conscience is the building block for a Christian's walk with the Lord. Without the conscience there is no walk. This is evident in the following verses taken from the New English Translation:

> I put this charge before you, Timothy my child, in keeping with the prophecies once spoken about you, in order that with such encouragement you may fight the good fight. To do this you must hold firmly to faith and a good conscience, which some have rejected and so have suffered shipwreck in regard to the faith. Among these are Hymenaeus and Alexander, whom I handed over to Satan to be taught not to blaspheme.[2]
> —1 TIMOTHY 1:18–20

In the above verses we see that some people had put away their conscience. What happened after that was their faith went down—it was shipwrecked. Their whole Christian life became shipwrecked because they had no testimony of the conscience.

HOLDING A PURE CONSCIENCE

There are people everywhere who have put away following their conscience. Before too long they stop assembling themselves—they backslide for a while, and before they know it, divorce comes into their home and their whole life comes apart.

Our conscience is meant to bring us to the Holy Spirit. Without the conscience there is no anchor in our life. Without the conscience there is no leading of the Holy Spirit. The job of the conscience is to help keep us clean and present us clean before the Lord. When we have guilt from our conscience talking to us on a certain matter, we cannot expect to have a clean conscience before the Lord or expect His blessings or guidance. We must first get right with Him in obeying our conscience. Then He is able to bless and guide us in all things.

> Likewise must the deacons be grave, not doubletongued, not given to much wine, not greedy of filthy lucre; Holding the mystery of the faith in a pure conscience.
> —1 TIMOTHY 3:8–9

What is Paul speaking of when he says "the mystery of the faith"? He is speaking about Christ in us, our hope of glory. It is the outworking of the total life of Christ in us. We are to hold our total life in Christ in a pure conscience.

I believe every Bible school should begin teaching their students about the conscience. They should know how easy it is to be Spirit-led and walking in the Word by their consciences. This would also stop the criticizing and the arguing. Instead of arguing about what God meant about this or that in His Word, people could save themselves a lot of time if they would listen to their consciences. The testimony of their consciences is a witness to the Word of God. But first, one needs to listen to what the conscience says.

How much more shall the blood of Christ, who through the eternal Spirit offered himself without spot to God, purge your conscience from dead works to serve the living God?

—HEBREWS 9:14

Before salvation we have an evil conscience toward God. Although we know right from wrong, our heart stiffens and hardens in a lost condition against God until the work of the Holy Spirit convicts us. When we accept Jesus as our Lord and Savior, our conscience is then completely washed in the blood of Jesus. It is cleansed and restored to its original position. We then begin our walk with the Lord having the Holy Spirit teaching us and our conscience.

FINDING THE CHRISTIAN'S NORMAL ENVIRONMENT

Having a good conscience; that, whereas they speak evil of you, as of evildoers, they may be ashamed that falsely accuse your good conversation in Christ. For it is better, if the will of God be so, that ye suffer for well doing, than for evil doing.

—1 PETER 3:16–17

In the scripture passage above Peter commands the church to have a good conscience. During this time the people of the church were under persecution and being falsely accused. The accusers knew they were telling lies concerning the church; however, the church was pure and righteous. Those who knew the people of the church had to say of a truth, "God is in you."

The ideal condition for any church is one of purity and righteousness, whether they are in persecution or not. Usually it is better for Christians to be in persecution because it will bring growth. Christians tend to get sloppy in the Spirit when they are not in persecution.

Have you ever noticed how beautiful a jellyfish is in the water? The minute you take him out of his environment and put him on the hot deck of a ship, the jellyfish flattens out. This is similar to what Christians do when they are out of their environment. Do you know what the normal environment for a Christian is? It is fighting the good fight of faith. When we get out of the fight we go to pieces. Our spiritual muscles relax, and we become very good at compromising with fear. Christians should be sharp, ready for battle, never compromising, and having a testimony of a good conscience before God and man.

> *God, I pray that I purge my conscience to dead works and that I may learn to walk in good conscience before man and You at all times. In Jesus' name. Amen.*

Chapter 11

THE CHRISTIAN CONSCIENCE

THE CONSCIENCE IS a fixed factor that pronounces right and wrong on our actions. In fact, it could be called a fixed, innate factor. Because God has renewed a Christian's conscience, the conscience has a definite, sacred, and abiding authority. The Lord uses a Christian conscience to bring that person into a walk of holiness, righteousness, and fellowship with Himself. Because the conscience is sacred, it is under divine control and receives full revelation from God. Our conscience always witnesses to the Word of God and is able to remember instantly what the Lord says. In Romans 2:13–16 we find that we will be judged according to how we answer our conscience:

> For not the hearers of the law are just before God, but the doers of the law shall be justified. For when the Gentiles, which have not the law, do by nature the things contained in the law, these, having not the law, are a law unto themselves: Which shew the work of the law written in their hearts, their conscience also bearing witness, and their thoughts the mean while accusing or else excusing one another; In the day when God shall judge the secrets of men by Jesus Christ according to my gospel.

Martin Luther referred to the Reformation as "the awakening of the conscience."[1] Before the Reformation, the Roman Catholic Church had forbidden people to read the Bible. The church taught the people tradition instead of the Bible. At some place they were taught the Word, but they were not allowed to judge the Word. The people were told what and what not to believe. The Reformation changed all of this. It brought an openness of the Word of God. More people received the Word, and they were allowed to judge the Word for themselves. No longer did they have to have a priest tell them whether something was right or not. They began to stand on the authority of the Lord's Word and their own conscience.

MOVEMENTS OF THE CONSCIENCE

If we enter into disobedience and sin against God, the conscience begins to do a work of conviction against us. It will bring us to repentance and getting right with the Lord. At the time the conscience comes against us, fellowship with the Lord is broken until we repent. In 1 Samuel 24:4-6, David's conscience came against him when his heart smote him for cutting off Saul's skirt. Again in 2 Samuel 24:10, David's conscience smote him for numbering Israel. David had sinned in each of these cases, and his conscience spoke to him and smote him.

In Genesis we see Adam's conscience convicting him for disobeying God and eating the fruit. The Bible says Adam was afraid and hid himself from the Lord. When the conscience convicts us, we are not able to be in the presence of the Lord. Our heart smites us and we know we are guilty for disobeying the Lord. Sin breaks our fellowship with the Lord.

THE LAMP OF YOUR SOUL

The Moffatt translation of Proverbs 20:27 says, "Man's conscience is the lamp of the eternal, flashing into his inner most soul."[2] The conscience always judges and gives judgment on our actions. Both the Holy Spirit and our conscience govern our actions. They teach, oversee, and guide us in what we say, think, and do. The conscience will tell us whether we are hearing the Holy Spirit, or a religious spirit or demon. The conscience is a witness to the Holy Spirit. God has made us to know right from wrong and good from evil.

Listening and obeying the conscience is the mark of a mature Christian. Until we obey the guidance of our conscience, we are still babes in Christ.

> And he saith unto them, Is it lawful to do good on the sabbath days, or to do evil? to save life, or to kill? But they held their peace. And when he had looked round about on them with anger, being grieved for the hardness of their hearts.
>
> —MARK 3:4–5

The people in the verse above knew right from wrong yet they overruled their consciences and caused their hearts to harden. The conscience becomes violated when we harden our hearts. Jesus was grieved because the people were not being honest. They were hypocrites, doing what was wrong in the name of the Lord. When a person hardens his or her heart against the conscience and what he or she knows is right, the conscience becomes violated. The conscience is out of step with God. Fellowship with the Lord is broken, and the person is not in right standing with Him.

The main function of our conscience is to show us how

to walk with God. It becomes our guide. Some people think the conscience is mostly negative in its guidance, that it is always saying "no" or "do not do that," but this is not true. The conscience shows us positively how to walk with the Lord. When we read and meditate on the Word, God renews our conscience so that we learn His ways and do accordingly. We receive sound advice from our conscience and not just, "no, stay away from that." Through God's Word and His Holy Spirit our conscience grows in maturity and speaks to us, "This is the way. Walk ye in it."

SPEAKING THE TRUTH

We are able to know instantly whether or not we are speaking truth. Paul says in Romans 9:1, "I say the truth in Christ, I lie not, my conscience also bearing me witness in the Holy Ghost." Paul is saying he knows it is truth he speaks because his conscience bears him witness in the Holy Spirit. He knows he is following the Holy Spirit because his conscience told him it was the Holy Spirit.

Some people follow religious devils and cause themselves problems, all because they do not listen to their conscience. They get into error. Turning away from the conscience causes our faith to become shipwrecked. Our entire faith in Christ is shipwrecked. In listening and obeying the conscience we are able to know if it is the Holy Spirit speaking or not, and we know when we hear truth or not. When our conscience bears witness in the Holy Spirit, we have peace and rest; the conscience is not accusing.

RESTORATION OF THE CONSCIENCE

When a person receives Jesus as Lord and Savior, he or she becomes born again and a new creation in Jesus Christ, restored to right standing with God through the saving blood of Jesus. Everything about the person, including his or her conscience, is washed and cleansed in the blood of Jesus.

> Having therefore, brethren, boldness to enter into the holiest by the blood of Jesus, By a new and living way, which he hath consecrated for us, through the veil, that is to say, his flesh; And having an high priest over the house of God; Let us draw near with a true heart in full assurance of faith, having our hearts sprinkled from an evil conscience, and our bodies washed with pure water.
> —HEBREWS 10:19–22

The blood of Jesus cleanses us completely. His blood cleanses our conscience and restores it so that it functions again. With a cleansed conscience we know and are able to do the will of God.

> A new heart also will I give you, and a new spirit will I put within you: and I will take away the stony heart out of your flesh, and I will give you an heart of flesh. And I will put my spirit within you, and cause you to walk in my statues, and ye shall keep my judgments, and do them.
> —EZEKIEL 36:26–27

We see in the above verses that with our cleansed conscience we know and are able to do the will of God because He has restored us point by point in all things. A cleansed conscience causes a person to grow and mature in Christ. The more we obey our conscience, the stronger it becomes until we have a terrific guidance in our conscience that leads us directly to the heart of God and His Holy

Spirit. It is a sad thing today that some people receive very little guidance. What happens is they do not obey their consciences; they are guilty of overriding the leading of their consciences.

God, I want to be Spirit-led and walk in obedience to my conscience. I ask You to help me enter into this life You have prepared for me. In Jesus' name. Amen.

Chapter 12

HOW TO USE YOUR CONSCIENCE

HAT AUTHORITY DOES our conscience carry? How much authority should we give our conscience? Our conscience has the authority of God as its foundation. *Righteousness* and *God* are the same words. *Holiness* and *God* are the same words. *Love* and *God* are the same words. God always does right. He is peace and joy. When God made us in His likeness and image, He made us with a conscience. In every way we are a concrete example of Him.

As Christians, we are being brought to the fullness of the stature of the Lord Jesus Christ. Through His saving blood our conscience has been washed and restored. Not obeying our conscience causes us to sin. The conscience will speak to us and convict us of our sin until we confess and ask forgiveness. Our conscience will not leave us alone until we confess. First John 1:9 says, "If we confess our sins, he is faithful and just to forgive us our sins, and to cleanse us from all unrighteousness."

Most Christians have no knowledge about the positive side of the conscience. The conscience not only asks us questions but also provides the answers. Everything we do should be done to the glory of the Lord, whether it is spiritual or not. When something is done well or done right, where do you think that uplifting feeling comes from? Likewise, where does that terrible low feeling come from when you slight your work? In both cases the conscience is speaking to you.

PURGE YOUR CONSCIENCE

The conscience in a Christian is very alert. It has been restored, cleansed, and washed in the blood of Jesus.

> How much more shall the blood of Christ, who through the eternal Spirit offered himself without spot to God, purge your conscience from dead works to serve the living God?
>
> —HEBREWS 9:14

Some Christians are not sure if their conscience or God or the devil is speaking to them. The conscience always bears witness in the Holy Spirit. Reading and meditating on God's Word causes any area in our conscience that may be seared to be cleansed and set right. His Word liberates a seared conscience. Disobeying the conscience causes us problems. It is important we always obey our conscience and get the Word of God in us. The Holy Spirit then takes the words of Jesus and makes them known unto us and shows us things that will shortly come to pass.

A clean conscience allows the Holy Spirit to speak to us. When we obey what the Spirit is saying, our conscience is a witness to the Spirit and the Spirit is a witness to our conscience. The two will uplift us when we obey and will convict us of sin when we disobey. The Holy Spirit guides us, while the conscience is the monitor that lets us know whether it is the Holy Spirit speaking or not.

How do we get rid of a seared conscience? Only God's written Word will do it. If a person is in sin and his conscience is not talking to him, he must get in the Word and see what the Lord says. As soon as the Word of God reaches a person, the conscience is healed. The blood of Jesus Christ washes him clean, and he has been renewed in the conscience. Only God and His Word can heal a seared conscience.

Father, I honor You. All honor, glory, and majesty belong to You. From the depths of my heart I give myself to You to be the fit minister of Your life. Cause the Word You have placed within me to grow and cause me to mature in all things in accordance to Your Word. I thank You, Father, for the Word You have given me. Keep me in the fellowship of Your Spirit. In Jesus' name. Amen.

Chapter 13

DEALING WITH THE
DOUBTFUL CONSCIENCE

ACH OF US runs into things we are unsure of and have doubt about. There are those people who do not believe some things in the Word. But we must walk right at all times in the Lord. In Romans 14 we are called to make decisions concerning doubtful things. Paul writes that God at one time made a distinction between clean and unclean. To this day there are people who will not eat pork or worship on any other day but Saturday. A person can be a good Christian and convince others that eating pork or worshiping on Sunday are wrong.

> I know, and am persuaded by the Lord Jesus, that there is nothing unclean of itself: but to him that esteemeth any thing to be unclean, to him it is unclean.
> —ROMANS 14:14

People who try to convince others they should eat a certain food or worship only on a certain day are stealing the victory a person has through Jesus Christ. Doing so brings bondage, depression, or oppression.

SETTLE IT NOW

I recommend that those who are in ministry read all of chapter fourteen in the book of Romans. This chapter is a study that should be settled in our hearts before we minister to other people. The weak brethren have problems like those mentioned in the chapter. They give themselves to carnal things. Paul writes that we are not to cause our brother to stumble:

> Who art thou that judgest another man's servant? to his own master he standeth or falleth. Yea, he shall be holden up: for God is able to make him stand.
> —ROMANS 14:4

In the verse above, Paul says we are not to judge those who are free in Christ. But it seems we do judge our brother and we do not even consider it sin. But God does. Judging our brother in Christ only stops the flow of fellowship with the Lord. This verse also shows us there are two classes of believers. There are the weak and the strong. You will never find a congregation that is all weak or all strong. Every assembly has the pious and weak brother who sits back and judges others who are free in the Lord and know that nothing is unclean. Believers who have the revelation that nothing is unclean will walk according to their consciences, the Word, and the Holy Spirit. It is a greater thing to walk in the Spirit than it is to walk in the Law.

Those who are strong in the Lord are not to destroy the weak, and the weak are not to judge the strong. Whether we are strong or weak, we must always have a good conscience before God and not allow doubtful things to rob us of our liberty in Christ.

HAPPY IS HE WHO CONDEMNS NOT

> Hast thou faith? have it to thyself before God. Happy is he that condemeth not himself in that thing which he alloweth.
>
> —ROMANS 14:22

The faith spoken of in this verse is not the Christian faith or the gift of faith. It is the faith to be free—to be strong. God does not want us covered with fleshly hang-ups or legalism. This is a faith that accepts God's revelation. When a person is hung up on the law as a restriction, they are unable to enter into God's rest. Having the faith that Paul speaks about in this verse allows the restrictions to be removed from the things that were formerly forbidden by the law.

Our conscience accepts the Word of God, but traditions overrule the conscience. One time there was a minister who gave communion in a church using real wine instead of grape juice. Several of the dear old women got fighting mad and blew up. They nearly tore the minister apart. They were mad because they had signed a pledge in the Methodist Church that said they would never touch alcohol. They had a tradition that cannot be found in the New Testament. It overruled their consciences.

> For meat destroy not the work of God. All things indeed are pure; but it is evil for that man who eateth with offence.
>
> —ROMANS 14:20

> For the kingdom of God is not meat and drink; but righteousness, and peace, and joy in the Holy Ghost.
>
> —ROMANS 14:17

If you have problems in legalistic things or if people judge and condemn you for what you eat or drink, read Romans 14 over and over. Know that those who condemn you live by a standard and tradition that is all their own. They do not understand their freedom in Christ because of their judging. But the Bible also tells us not to offend such as these. We are not to condemn our brother who is free or look down on those who are not free in Christ.

Lord God, help me to deal with doubts and stay free as I walk and live in a good conscience. In Jesus' name. Amen.

Chapter 14

THE INDWELLING SPIRIT WORKING WITHIN

OBEDIENCE TO OUR conscience is the first step to becoming Spirit-led. The next step is knowing how the Holy Spirit continues to work in us. The glory of God is His holiness. The Lord hates and destroys evil and loves and blesses the good. We in turn will condemn sin and will approve righteousness through the working of the Spirit within us. Our conscience is in touch with the very holiness of God.

The work of our conscience is to witness to our being right or wrong with God. When we are right with God we know He accepts our faith because of the witness we receive from our conscience and the Holy Spirit. There is a difference in the way the conscience and the Holy Spirit witness. The conscience tells us we are right with God. The Spirit of God gives us a deep-down, settled knowing that God has accepted our faith. Eventually the conscience and the Spirit will merge into one strong voice. But first the conscience must be taught. There is work to be done on the conscience of man before he can completely line up with the Spirit of God.

"I say the truth in Christ, I lie not, my conscience also bearing me witness in the Holy Ghost" (Rom. 9:1). We see that Paul has come to a position where his conscience works in the Holy Spirit. Together they have one voice instead of

113

two. The time comes when the conscience and the Holy Spirit blend together and become perfectly joined in one because they agree with the Word.

The Bible tells us that God's laws are written on our hearts. When we sin, the light that is within the Word written on our hearts manifests. It shines in us and lights up that sin, making it manifest itself. This convicts us of our sin. If we do not confess that sin, the conscience becomes defiled and we no longer are able to hear the voice of God.

> Unto the pure all things are pure: but unto them that are defiled and unbelieving is nothing pure; but even their mind and conscience is defiled.
>
> —TITUS 1:15

In the verses below, Paul is writing to Christians about Christians:

> For there are many unruly and vain talkers and deceivers, specially they of the circumcision: whose mouths must be stopped, who subvert whole houses, teaching things which they ought not, for filthy lucre's sake. One of themselves, even a prophet of their own, said, The Cretians are always liars, evil beasts, slow bellies. This witness is true.
>
> —TITUS 1:10–13

Paul is talking about those who came and ministered as elders in the assembly. These people were recognized as elders but their consciences had become defiled. What happens when a person's conscience is defiled? Instead of being Spirit-led, something else happens. The next verse tells us what it is that happens.

They profess that they know God; but in works they deny him, being abominable, and disobedient, and unto every good work reprobate.

—Titus 1:16

If our conscience is defiled, it makes no difference what we say with our mouth. Our life will go the other direction. Our life becomes unstable, and we are unable to walk in the Word. A defiled conscience separates us from being led by God to walk in His Word. We must be led of the Spirit of God to walk in victory.

THE THREE-PHASE WORK OF THE HOLY SPIRIT

The Holy Spirit works in our conscience in three phases. Each phase brings us into a closer spiritual walk with God. In the first phase the Holy Spirit causes the light of the Word to shine in our heart. When conviction by the Word comes to the conscience and we respond to that conviction, we are delivered. We are saved and set free. The light of the Word restores the working of the conscience. It begins to function again in the light of God's Word. This is the first phase.

The second phase can only happen when the first phase is complete. In the second phase the Spirit cleanses the conscience. It is one thing to have a conscience but another to have one that is cleansed. We see that first the Spirit convicts us of sin so that we can be delivered and set free. Then He begins cleansing the conscience. The Spirit uses the blood of Jesus to wash out all defilement and to wake it up to testify to God's Word. The conscience will always testify, "Thus saith the Lord." The cleansed conscience always brings forth God's

Word. So we see that first the illuminating and bringing a spark causes us to come to Christ. When we are in Christ, the blood of Jesus cleanses the conscience. The third phase in the work of the Holy Spirit is in keeping our conscience clean by the blood of Jesus.

> For our rejoicing is this, the testimony of our conscience, that in simplicity and godly sincerity, not with fleshly wisdom, but by the grace of God, we have had our conversation in the world, and more abundantly to you-ward.
>
> —2 CORINTHIANS 1:12

The testimony of our conscience is kept clean by our living and obeying the Word. Through this the Holy Spirit keeps us clean. The Holy Spirit uses our conscience to bring us into complete obedience to Christ. The Spirit uses the conscience so much that when it is cleansed and obedient, the conscience blends together with the Holy Spirit. When we are in good conscience before God we are then Spirit-led. Keeping a cleansed conscience and being Spirit-led causes us to trust our conscience completely in bringing us into a total walk with God in the Spirit. The conscience and the Spirit become one voice.

Everyone wants to be filled with the Holy Spirit, but there are some who do not want to obey their consciences. Being filled with the Holy Spirit means we must be obedient to the Word, having a good and pure conscience—one that is open at all times to "thus saith the Lord." When this happens, the infilling of the Spirit will come, and we will be filled to constant overflowing by the Holy Spirit.

Father God, may the simplicity of the faith be mine, that I not have a shipwrecked faith, but a good faith and a good conscience walking in obedience. In Jesus' name. Amen.

Chapter 15
RESTORATION OF THE CHURCH

E ALL KNOW the time we are living in. We are living in the last of the Last Days according to the Word of God. A day is as a thousand years with the Lord. We see this in the seven days of the Lord and in the seven days of Creation. The past two thousand years are the end of the sixth day. The seventh day that is coming will be the kingdom age; the age of peace on Earth—the age of rest.

The time we live in today is still the day of the Gentiles. We are still in the time of Jacob's troubles. It is a time in which there are wars and rumors of wars; a time that Christians should become the manifested sons of God. We also see there must be a restoration of the church. When we talk about the restoration of the church, we all say "amen," until we stop and think that as Christians we *are* the church. This means we have to be restored to what God really wants us to be. He wants us to be like Jesus—the first-born among many co-equal brethren.

Many people think the church will not be restored simply because they know they are not restored. But it is the work of the Holy Spirit. Also it is the work of the body of Christ, the work of the five-fold ministry. It is the work of everyone who is being restored to help each other. We must be made ready to function in the body of Christ.

Have you ever studied the book of Song of Solomon? Solomon is the one who is restoring the Shulamite. She is the church. What is happening today is evident in the Song of Solomon. We see in many places in that book where the church is being restored. The Shulamite loses track of the Lord once in a while and likewise Christians today lose track of the Lord and wander out into the world.

GOD DEALS WITH HIS BODY

You and I must be made ready to function in the body of Christ. This is why belonging to a local church is so necessary. In Hebrew 10:25 the Lord says, "Not forsaking the assembling of ourselves together, as the manner of some is; but exhorting one another: and so much the more, as ye see the day approaching." God deals with His body, and to do this He deals with individuals. He deals with each one of us. It takes the body of Christ to bless the world. It takes the body of Christ rising up as one in unity. When the church begins to walk in their position, it is like Jesus has come to town. This is what restoration is all about. The Lord is then able to minister in the way He wants to minister.

Today it seems that many Christians do not have that inner urge to be developed into the fullness of the stature of Christ. But this is the call of God for today, that we be developed to the fullness of the stature of Christ. For you and me to live is Christ—not a fake, not an imitation, but as Christ, the Anointed One.

> For as the body is one, and hath many members, and all the members of that one body, being many, are one body: so also is Christ.
>
> —1 CORINTHIANS 12:12

120

Paul writes about different members quarreling with each other to the point the body is unable to function as it should. We know that individual parts of the body can function, similar to a car that does not have a motor but does have tires that could allow you to push it around anyway. This is what is going on in the church today. It is mostly soul power. It is mostly people trying to get programs moving instead of being led by the Holy Spirit of God. Each day we should ask God to fill us with His Holy Spirit. We do not have to wait around for a great, thrilling experience. Jesus said if we ask Him, He will do it. This is a tremendous thing. We will see a big difference in our lives, whether we feel it or not.

God is not interested in what we feel. He is interested in what we are. When we make room for the Holy Spirit, with room for the gifts to operate and for everyone to come forth into their ministry, it should be easy for the church to function.

THE SCHOOL OF THE SPIRIT

I have had many pastors say to me, "Bill, you have a dangerous church. You actually let other people in the pulpit? You actually let them prophesy without telling you first what they are going to say?" I believe it is the Lord, and if it is not, then I will tell that person. The Bible says to let others judge prophecy. It is not dangerous. I want the Holy Spirit to have first place in our church. He is God. Let Him be God in your life and in the church service. We must be perfected in our ministry, and because of this we have a school of the Spirit on Wednesday nights. The school allows you to come forth in your prophecy, healings, or whatever God has called you to do.

In our services, people's revelation can come forth because

they put it into practice. They learn by faith and the power of God's Word. I want each person to come forth in revelation and each individual to come forth in their calling. God is going to restore the church, and we have to make ourselves available to the Holy Spirit for this to happen. If we do not, the first time the Holy Spirit asks us to do something we are not used to doing, we may end up having an inner battle with ourselves. It could be similar to an experience I had as a young boy.

As a small boy I worked for a farmer. I took the cows into the barn to milk them. One day I took them into the wrong stall, and the cows were really unhappy about that. The farmer told me, "We're not going to get milk until you change those cows around. They are mad at you and won't let their milk down." It is the same thing when God takes us out of the stall we have been in all our lives. When He puts us in His stall, we start to throw a fit for a while until we come into obedience to the Holy Spirit.

Prophecy to the Church

Thus saith the Lord:

I am making a change. I am making it fast and I am making it quick. For you shall be changed and you shall say, "Lord God, what have you done to me?" And I will say, "This is the way I have for you. Walk ye in it and you shall be blessed of Me."

KNOW THE WILL OF GOD

Is your heart real? Is your life real? Or is it someplace else rather than in God?

I beseech you therefore, brethren, by the mercies of God, that ye present your bodies a living sacrifice, holy, acceptable unto God, which is your reasonable service. And be not conformed to this world: but be ye transformed by the renewing of your mind, that ye may prove what is that good, and acceptable, and perfect, will of God.

—ROMANS 12:1–2

Now think about this. Most people do not know the will of God. Most do not hear the voice of God, and I believe I know why this is. We do not have to wonder what the will of God is if we do what He wants us to do. We must want the will of God more than we want the will of the world. Some people try to pick and choose which parts of the world they want. But it does not work this way.

WALKING IN THE WORD

We have seen in earlier chapters how a conscience can become seared when it accepts a lie as if it were the truth. A seared conscience is one that does not hear guidance on certain things of the Lord. This is why some people will say, "Tongues are of the devil." Their conscience is seared in this area. When the Lord deals with them they will see the truth. To set the conscience right, a person must act upon the Word of God whether they have any feeling about it or not. The Word of God is true, and if it says something that your conscience is not speaking to you about, act on God's Word anyway. When we act on His Word by faith, the conscience is released to obey. It is able to speak to us in the area in which it was previously seared.

We must remember that in order for us to walk in the Spirit we must first obey our conscience. We must come to a place of obeying God's Word simply because it is God's Word. I believe the first step in the restoration of the church

123

is in the restoration of our conscience. If we refuse truth, how can we be restored? If we refuse truth, our conscience will not tell us, "Amen. This is the way. Walk ye in it."

The conscience has so much to do with our walk. It will tell us yes or no, and it will tell us "go left" or "go right." Our conscience was placed within us by God Himself. Listening to and obeying our conscience is the first step in being led by His Holy Spirit.

EXERCISE THYSELF IN THE HOLY SPIRIT

> And herein do I exercise myself, to have always a conscience void of offence toward God, and toward men.
>
> —ACTS 24:16

Do you remember in the Bible when David was on a rooftop and watched Bathsheba take a bath? He then brought her into the palace and committed adultery with her. A year passed before he was once again right before the Lord. Until that time his conscience bothered him constantly. David prayed, "Restore unto me the Holy Spirit." David began begging God. But his conscience was not free until he confessed his sin. If you are in sin and your conscience *is not* bothering you, you have accepted the sin as righteous—and sin is not righteousness. Friendship with the world is enmity with God. When you make friends with the world you begin to pick and choose what is good and bad instead of obeying the Word of God. You need your conscience set free.

> I say the truth in Christ, I lie not, my conscience also bearing me witness in the Holy Ghost.
>
> —ROMANS 9:1

Some people say, "I don't know if this is God or not." When the conscience is set free it tells us whether it is the Holy Spirit or not. The conscience guides us into all truth. If a person has a seared conscience, he will argue with the truth. Here is an example: the Greek language Bible uses the word *indecorium* describing a man having long hair. The word *indecorium* refers to a violation of God's rule of conduct. But when you talk to a man who has long hair and tell him he should cut it, you will be in for a fight. It does not matter how big a Christian he is because he is in love with that hair. The man with long hair will fight for that long hair instead of the rule of conduct that God wants men to live by.

AGREE WITH THE WORD

If we are going to be restored, we have to agree with the Lord and His Word. There are many places we are not in agreement with the Lord and His Word. The reason is that the conscience is seared and it does not bother us. My wife and I have made it a habit in life of trying to keep our conscience free. Because of this many people think we are living back in the forties. What we want is to be living in righteousness. Think about the television shows and the filth that is being taught as right. Many consciences are being seared. Think about what is going on in the school systems today. From grade one on up they are teaching about sex, but the students graduate without knowing how to read or write. People defend these things because their consciences are seared in those areas. Their consciences no longer talk to them about it because they have accepted a lie as truth.

For our rejoicing is this, the testimony of our conscience, that in simplicity and godly sincerity, not

125

with fleshly wisdom, but by the grace of God, we have had our conversation in the world, and more abundantly to you-ward.

—2 CORINTHIANS 1:12

Their conscience says, "You're OK in what you are doing." But if it is not right, God will forgive and cleanse them if they repent and seek forgiveness. We also must act upon the Word to be set free. This is called walking by faith. Asking God to forgive us is part of the way there. The rest of the way requires that we repent of the sin. Repentance means to turn around and go the other direction, to walk away from it. Restoration is impossible if we refuse to be restored.

Someone asked me one time why the stations of the cross are not in our church. We purposely make it impossible for anyone to worship anything else other than Jesus. We do not want anyone to worship icons. Worship nothing but the Lord God Himself. That is what it is all about.

RESTORING OUR CONSCIENCE

We have seen that we cannot be restored as a church until our conscience is restored.

Ye adulterers and adulteresses, know ye not that the friendship of the world is enmity with God? whosoever therefore will be a friend of the world is the enemy of God.

—JAMES 4:4

The verse above is a very hard word because many Christians have already accepted the world as their friend and have let homosexuals set their dress code, for example. It is a hard thing for a Christian woman to go buy a dress she can wear decently. Some believe if the world does it, it must be OK for the church. The world has moved into the church so much that if we were to preach what we do here in an average church, we would be asked to leave. The spirit of the world has taken over some churches. The spirit of the world is the spirit that governs lost people. This same spirit is the one that causes people to buy what they do not need and run up their credit cards on things for which they have no use. When the Bible says, "Owe no man nothing but love," it does not mean Christians are not allowed to charge something. It means we should never charge so much that we cannot pay for it. You do not owe it until it is due. Do you see?

My wife and I know a couple that got a ten-thousand-dollar Christmas bonus every year. One time on New Year's Day they came around to visit and said, "We got it done!" We knew they were three months behind on their house payments. I asked, "Did you catch up on your house payments?" They said, "Oh no, that's not Christmas." They threw the money away. Year after year they would do this. They had no control on their finances. God wants us to control our finances in faithful, obedient stewardship of His provision.

We must remember that we are to free our conscience on every subject that it has been seared. Sometimes it may be small things. Some say, "I have the gift of prophecy, but I can't prophesy in a crowd." This is a lie, of course. To be able to prophesy in a crowd, you have to act upon it. Ask God to forgive you for disobedience, then act in faith. Whatever God is telling you to do, you should act on it. If you do not, before long you will say He is wrong and you are right. When you do that you have accepted the lie. Your conscience will not speak to you. We must be free, and we as the church must be ready. We must obey the Lord each time He speaks. But if the conscience does not speak, how can we know if it is the Lord?

WALKING IN THE WILL OF GOD

I beseech you therefore, brethren, by the mercies of God, that ye present your bodies a living sacrifice, holy, acceptable unto God, which is your reasonable service. And be not conformed to this world: but be ye transformed by the renewing of your mind, that ye may prove what is that good, and acceptable, and perfect, will of God.

—ROMANS 12:1–2

The Greek translation for the phrase *to be transfigured* is the same word used for the Transfiguration. It means to be transfigured into the full stature of Christ once we have done the things it says Romans 12:1–2. We must walk in the will of God at all times. The enemy will tell you that people are in legalism when they follow God's Word to the letter. But I like to see the dead raised, see miracles, and see signs and wonders. Keeping our conscience clean so we can hear the voice of the Lord will cause us to see all of these.

I like to go in front of many people I have never seen before and say, "Thus saith the Lord, the Word of God for you," and tell them exactly what God is talking to them about. It blesses my heart. I thank God daily for this gifting.

When we were in Europe ministering at the Forming and Action Pentecostal Bible School, I went one by one to each student and told them what God called them to do and to be. They received a true Word of the Lord. To do this you need to have a clear conscience. If your conscience is disagreeing with the Word of God, it needs to be set free. You need to start acting upon what is in the Word of God. Trust your conscience. Trust the Holy Spirit. He will tell you the truth and only the truth. When you trust the Holy Spirit and act upon what He says, your conscience is then set free little by little. You do not get it just like that. It is every subject on everything that the Word of God teaches.

THE RESTORED CHURCH

I see the church today being restored and then I see so many churches heading off toward the left or the right. They do not stay in the Word. This is what we have to watch for.

When we have weddings in our church they are centered around Jesus. Not frills. Jesus. There are some frills, but they do not distract from the Lord Himself. We want Him to be the Hub of the service. Jesus says, "For where two or three are gathered together in my name, there am I in the midst of them" (Matt. 18:20).

I cannot stress enough the importance of trusting your conscience. If you have things in your life that are not according to the Word of God, ask Him to forgive you. Only then will your conscience be set free.

This should take place in many parts of our lives. None of us have a truly free conscience at this time. God will start dealing with us point by point to set us free. Our conscience will speak to us. I want that kind of life. I want a transparent life. I want a life in which my conscience functions as God wants it to function. I want the Spirit of God's voice to be loud and fellowship with Him to be closer than close. All of this is possible because He sets the conscience free.

As our conscience is being restored, we are becoming restored in every area of our life until we can say from the heart, "For to me to live is Christ, and to die is gain" (Phil. 1:21). This is what it is all about.

129

Would you like to get your conscience set free? Simply accept the Word of God. Doing this is not legalism as some have said.

Prophecy to the Church

Thus saith the Lord:

I have called, I have called, and I have called. You have come to Me, but you have not given your all. For I, the Lord God, would say unto My people, this is the day that you shall make up your mind and decide that you will walk with Me in Spirit and in truth. For if you walk with Me in Spirit, you must walk with Me in truth, and the truth will set you free. For this truth I give unto you. I have come to heal what the enemy has destroyed. I have come to set in place what the enemy has torn down. I have come to put the foundation in your life that will make it possible for you to live as a manifested son of God.

Heavenly Father, I give myself to You this day to have my conscience set free, that I might be led of the Holy Spirit and my conscience into the fullness of Your Word. I accept this by faith because Your Word tells me if I pray in Your will, You hear me. And if I know that You hear me, I know I receive the answer. So I thank You, Lord, for restoring my conscience. In Jesus' name. Amen.

NOTES

Chapter 1
Your God-given Conscience

1. Web site: www.absolutelyhonest.com/authors/
Martin%20Luther_quotes.html, accessed January 26, 2009.

2. Henry Edward Archbishop of Westminster, *The Demon of Socrates*, paper read before the Royal Institution (January 26, 1872), http://www.scribd.com/doc/3190613/The-Demon-of-Socrates-, accessed March 4, 2009.

3. James Strong, ed., *Strong's Exhaustive Concordance of the Bible*, (Nashville, TN: Thomas Nelson Publishers, 1997), s.v. "4893" and "4894."

Chapter 3
The Revelation of the Conscience

1. Web site: http://www.goodreads.com/author/quotes/29874 .Martin_Luther, accessed January 26, 2009.

2. James Moffatt, *A New Translation of the Bible, Containing the Old and New Testaments* (New York: Doran, 1926), revised edition, (New York and London: Harper and Brothers, 1935), reprinted, (Grand Rapids, MI: Kregel, 1995).

3. Web site: http://www.goodreads.com/author/quotes/29874 .Martin_Luther, accessed January 26, 2009.

Chapter 5
The Secret Authority

1. Web site: www.absolutelyhonest.com/authors/
Martin%20Luther_quotes.html, accessed January 26, 2009.

Chapter 6
Association with Actions

1. "Old Testament Hebrew Lexicon," StudyLight.org, s.v. "6754," http://www.studylight.org/lex/heb/view.cgi?number=06754, accessed March 4, 2009.

CHAPTER 8
FOLLOWING OUR CONSCIENCE

1. Web site: www.absolutelyhonest.com/authors/ Martin%20Luther_quotes.html, accessed January 26, 2009.

CHAPTER 9
KNOWING MORAL VALUE

1. James Strong, ed., *Strong's Exhaustive Concordance of the Bible*, (Nashville, TN: Thomas Nelson Publishers, 1997).

CHAPTER 10
OBEYING THE CHECKS AND BALANCES

1. John Bunyan, *Holy War* (New Kensington, PA: Whitaker House, 1985).

2. New English Translation passage sourced from Web site: www .bible.org/netbible/index.htm, accessed January 26, 2009.

CHAPTER 11
THE CHRISTIAN CONSCIENCE

1. Web site: www.archive.org/stream/ historyofreformat186301merl/historyofreformat186301merl_djvu.txt, accessed January 26, 2009.

2. James Moffatt, *A New Translation of the Bible, Containing the Old and New Testaments* (New York: Doran, 1926), revised edition, (New York and London: Harper and Brothers, 1935), reprinted, (Grand Rapids, MI: Kregel, 1995).

To Contact the Author

drbillsmith@cebridge.net